T0318496

# Cambridge Elements ≡

**Elements in Public Policy**
edited by
M. Ramesh
*National University of Singapore (NUS)*
Michael Howlett
*Simon Fraser University, British Colombia*
Xun WU
*Hong Kong University of Science and Technology*
Judith Clifton
*University of Cantabria*
Eduardo Araral
*National University of Singapore (NUS)*

# RELATIONALITY

## *The Inner Life of Public Policy*

Raul P. Lejano
*New York University*

Wing Shan Kan
*Hong Kong Baptist University*

Shaftesbury Road, Cambridge CB2 8EA, United Kingdom

One Liberty Plaza, 20th Floor, New York, NY 10006, USA

477 Williamstown Road, Port Melbourne, VIC 3207, Australia

314–321, 3rd Floor, Plot 3, Splendor Forum, Jasola District Centre, New Delhi – 110025, India

103 Penang Road, #05–06/07, Visioncrest Commercial, Singapore 238467

Cambridge University Press is part of Cambridge University Press & Assessment, a department of the University of Cambridge.

We share the University's mission to contribute to society through the pursuit of education, learning and research at the highest international levels of excellence.

www.cambridge.org
Information on this title: www.cambridge.org/9781009113199

DOI: 10.1017/9781009118996

First published 2022

*A catalogue record for this publication is available from the British Library.*

ISBN 978-1-009-11319-9 Paperback
ISSN 2398-4058 (online)
ISSN 2514-3565 (print)

# Relationality

## The Inner Life of Public Policy

Elements in Public Policy

DOI: 10.1017/9781009118996
First published online: November 2022

Raul P. Lejano
*New York University*

Wing Shan Kan
*Hong Kong Baptist University*

**Author for correspondence:** Raul P. Lejano, lejano@nyu.edu

**Abstract:** This Element argues that relational policy analysis can provide deeper insights into the career of any policy and the dynamics of any policy situation. This task is all the more difficult as the relational often operates unseen in the backstages of a policy arena. Another issue is the potentially unbounded scope of a relational analysis. But these challenges should not dissuade policy scholars from beginning to address the theme of relationality in public policy. This Element sketches a conceptual framework for the study of relationality and illustrates some of the promise of relational analysis using an extended case study. This title is also available as Open Access on Cambridge Core.

**Keywords:** relationality, relational policy analysis, policy design, implementation, network governance

ISBNs: 9781009113199 (PB), 9781009118996 (OC)
ISSNs: 2398-4058 (online), 2514-3565 (print)

# Contents

# 1 Introduction: Relationality in the Policy Domain

The central theme of this Element is the relational dimension of policy life. How does the web of relationships among policy actors affect the construction and conduct of policy? How might we approach the task of conceptualizing, then discerning, the nature and action of the relational?

One can dismiss the task by simply saying that relationships are everything and everywhere. You might as well study how molecules influence policy, somebody might say. But other concepts used for analysis are similarly ubiquitous and unbounded, for example, beliefs, narrative, discourse, and rationality. The ubiquity and unboundedness of the relational should not dissuade us from building policy theories around it and crafting new ways of studying it. What is needed is to operationalize the concept of relationality for the purpose of deepening policy analysis. Scholars and practitioners both should begin the task of discovering aspects of relationality that can be analyzed and that are useful for their theory and practice. As importantly, we should be accumulating a store of case studies that illustrate relationality in policy life, building an array of examples of analysis.

One reason (but not the only one) for formally addressing the relational is to better understand policy anomalies. Anomalies abound in policy life, where things are not as they are intended to be (e.g., Carstensen, 2015; Wilder and Howlett, 2015). In one city, a formal schedule of property taxes is routinely deviated from, and payments are instead negotiated with assessors on a case-to-case basis. In another, a public-school charter that aims for a consistent level of quality everywhere gives way to a system where differing communities, with differing levels of income and influence, lobby to get better schools. In one state, a blanket public health measure requiring face masks is embraced in some districts and flouted in others.

The analyst can classify these as anomalies, call for better implementation, and leave it at that. But it is much more informative to take a more phenomenological view. This entails letting go of the urge to classify policy situations as normal or deviant and, instead, to describe and analyze them as they are. The early phenomenologist, Husserl, described a mode of description that brackets away strong assumptions about what a thing is or should be and, instead, returns "to the things themselves" (Husserl, 1900/1901, 168). This can require attending more faithfully to the complexity of a situation, what Geertz referred to as "thick description" (Geertz, 1973, 5).

One conventional way to view policy is as prescription – that is, as a plan for achieving good public ends.[1] This is corollary to a conventional view of policy

---

[1] The authors wish to assure the reader that there is no intent to evoke an instrumental/purposive notion of policy. In fact, it is always tempting to use the straw figure of the rational model as an

as problem-solving (as noted by Turnbull, 2006). As Wildavsky wrote early on, "Policies are goals, objectives, and missions that guide the agency. Analysis evaluates and sifts alternative means and ends in the elusive pursuit of policy recommendations" (Wildavsky, 1964, 29). But, as Wildavsky and others later demonstrated, there may be gaps between the plan and its enactment because of the vagaries of implementation. Often, policy seems to invariably obey a different logic, repurposed if you will. Some suggest that policy actors behave according to a logic of appropriateness (March and Olsen, 1989), but the question is: Appropriateness to what? Some allude to a more informal, transactional policy of "nondesign" (Howlett and Mukherjee, 2014) but, again, we wonder: What is the logic of nondesign? We need to better describe these logics or mechanisms that seem to drive public policy in opaque, unintended, or informal ways. In this Element, we propose to trace these inner logics to relational phenomena. We will refer to this as a model of *relationality* in public policy (Lejano, 2021).

> Within the realm of public policy research, the term *relationality* pertains to the generative role that relationships have in shaping and enacting policy. *Relationality* is the condition in which policy, in its meanings and practice, emerges not just from formal, prescribed rulemaking and institution-building but also from the working and reworking of relationships among a network of policy actors.

In this Element, we will elaborate on the model of relationality and demonstrate how a relational framework can be used for policy analysis. A relational approach, as will be discussed, is useful not just for analyzing anomalies in public policy but in conventional policy situations as well. Later in this discussion, we sketch the outlines of how the relational approach might be useful in a prescriptive sense, in addition to its use for analysis.

In this provisional definition, we describe relationality not only as a condition but also as a set of processes. Relationships are mechanisms, operative among a web of policy actors, that generate policy. A relational analysis should aspire to a thick description of these mechanisms and their effect on policy.

## 1.1 Filling Gaps

A focus on the relational addresses gaps in several lines of research. We previously pointed to the literature on implementation as a body of knowledge built around policy anomalies – that is, when policy as realized departs from

---

ideological construct from which the relational perspective contrasts (as a pedagogic strategy). For those scholars who are wont to delineate orthodoxies within the field, the relational perspective could readily be considered as part of an interpretive turn in policy studies.

policy as intended. This dovetails well with a parallel literature on how implementation revolves around decisions made by "street-level bureaucrats," referring to agents of the state in the field who directly implement policies and interact with policy recipients (Lipsky, 1980). This discussion does not rest on the rather artificial boundaries drawn, historically, between policy formulation and implementation, but the focus on implementation (as a mode of coproduction of policy) is a useful pedagogic tool for illustrating the value of a relational perspective. So being, we enter into the discussion of relationality initially from a previous literature's focus on the street-level agent. Otherwise, the notion of relationality is a more general concept that is not particularly tied to the idea of or literature on implementation.

An open question in the scholarship around street-level agents is how to understand (and characterize) the kinds of decisions made at this level and how to account for the variation in patterns and outcomes of policy implementation (e.g., Winter, 2001). A body of literature has emerged around trying to explain decisions by the street-level bureaucrat as rational, involving maximizing individual utility or program outcomes (see the discussion in Chang, 2021). A variation of this involves an embedded assumption of bounded rationality, where the street-level agent adopts coping strategies, where policy targets are aimed for while dealing with organizational and resource constraints found at the field level (e.g., Ellis, 2011). These perspectives often view the street-level bureaucrat as an autonomous agent, making decisions and taking actions based on an individualistic logic operating under local constraints. But variations in decisions and outcomes are wide, and the literature attempts to explain this by correlating with individual-level characteristics such as demographic variables, self-perception, values, and so on (e.g., Wilkins and Williams, 2009).

However, as we will discuss in Section 2, there is considerable evidence by now, from fields such as social psychology and experimental economics, that decision-making has a strong relational component – that is, people make judgments not just as the rational individual but also as the connected individual responding to connections to the other. In short, to fully explain how street-level bureaucrats (and other policy actors) implement policy, we have to add the motivating factors induced by their being embedded in a web of relationships that guide their actions. Often, these decisions and actions depart from any semblance of individual rationality. March and Olsen characterized modes of decision-making that operate outside the rational agent model as the "logic of appropriateness" and characterize the latter as a fitting of decisions to rules and roles (March and Olsen, 2010). But, again, missing in this promising line of inquiry is an appreciation of how "appropriateness" also includes a fidelity to the relationships that one is a part of. Role and identity, as we will discuss in Section 2, are wrapped up in one's web of relationships.

Not that the importance of relationships has evaded scholars' attention. Every so often, the value of the relational will be mentioned. Lipsky's original treatise on street-level bureaucrats discusses the importance of the agent's relationship and interaction with the client. For example, Van Parys and Struyven recognize how relationships matter by trying to classify interaction styles in simplistic, categorical ways such as supportive, controlling, and so on (Van Parys and Struyven, 2018). As Hill and Hupe suggest: "it is relevant how street-level bureaucrats deal not only with rules (the substantive dimension) but also with other actors (the relational dimension)" (Hill and Hupe, 2021, 226) – and yet, there is so far no concerted attempt to analyze relationships between policy actors in detail.[2] At the same time as scholars acknowledge the importance of the relational, almost none attempt to analyze and describe relationship in enough richness and use such rich description to better understand policy processes and outcomes. One exception is Peake and Forsyth (2022), who call for a wider use of ethnographic interviews with street-level agents to understand how their interactions and programmatic contexts intertwine. As we will discuss in Section 4, this approach is one effective way of getting at the nature of relationships that influences the policy agent's thinking and action. It is likely to be an important route to adding to our knowledge of what constitutes logics of appropriateness.

One promising route runs through the literature on network governance (e.g., O'Toole et al., 1997). This scholarship promotes the important idea that policy emerges not simply from individuals enacting it but from social networks of interconnected individuals (and groups) whose interactions construct policy. In trying to connect the characteristics and dynamics of the network to policy outcomes and program effectiveness, the literature has largely focused on two aspects: first, the structural configuration of the social network and, second, how the heterogeneous, often nonformalized, network is managed. In doing so, the network literature primarily depicts network ties in terms of presence or absence of connection (i.e., classic social network analysis amounts to characterizing a network as a matrix of ones and zeroes). What is lacking is a deeper knowledge of what constitutes a tie – beyond presence or absence, how can we describe such ties (which, in this Element, we will refer to as relationship)? So, a more explicitly relational analysis will allow an understanding of network processes that go beyond the structure of switch-like ties and into the nature of these

---

[2] Some notable examples (such as Nisar and Maroulis, 2017) often employ quantitative approaches to social network analysis.

connections, which may differ from node to node. This takes us beyond macro-level insights into the importance of actor centrality and into questions about what constitutes centrality and how it functions. Interestingly, when the network literature does look at how processes work up close, it mostly revolves around the same assumption of the individual actor engaging in strategic behavior (e.g., Klijn, 1997, 29). As we will discuss in Section 2, our knowledge of individual decision-making is deeper now, and we know that individuals also act in a more relational way. Moreover, focusing closely on the nature of relationships moves us from the what (which actors are central) to the how (why and how their centrality matters).

The scholarship on policy networks arose because of the complexity of processes by which many policies are enacted. As Klijn describes it: "Policy processes in networks are unpredictable and complex ... Many authors have tried to define these processes in typologies of strategies" (Klijn, 1997, 32). But these meta-level approaches to characterizing relationships in networks (creating typologies, describing the structure of the network) do not allow us to explain what happens with each particular actor interacting with another. The idea presented herein is that describing exactly what these interpersonal (and interorganizational) relationships are, using richer modes of description, can help us explain what policy outcomes emerge and why.

Close examination of the relational allows us to go beyond typological descriptions of how policy is implemented in ways varying with context. For example, the literature on clientelism and policy networks usually concentrates on one mode of relationship where certain clients are favored (or capture the state) so that they receive disproportionately more benefits from a policy. But there is a much richer spectrum of possible relationships between client and state (including adverse relationships that detract from the client's welfare, cooperative relationships where clients participate in policy interpretation, etc.), and we need to better describe exactly what these relationships are, how they function, and how these affect policy outcomes.

Relational phenomena are often found in the inner workings of policy – that is, behind the scenes and in ways not acknowledged by formal or codified policy. Such phenomena are relevant to all aspects of policy formulation/ enactment. They blur any notion of stages in the policy process and their recognition perhaps blends well with constructivist perspectives on policy-making that eschew the autonomous subject (see Barbehön, 2022, for a review). In this Element, we use the concept of relationality as a general framework for *policy analysis*, especially in evaluating how and why policies emerge and effect change (e.g., Lejano, 2021).

Across the broader landscape of policy studies, one can view relationality as part of the interpretive turn in policy scholarship. This can be understood in the same spirit as other studies' attempts to describe how policy is constructed through the interactions of multiple policy actors (e.g., Durose and Richardson, 2015). Focusing on relationality means understanding these interactions as, in part, expression of relationships among these actors. This draws inspiration from a related literature in the area of relational sociology, in which society is analyzed not as a static constellation of things or properties but dynamic, unfolding relations (e.g., Emirbayer, 1997; Powell and Dépelteau, 2013). As Donati writes, "society is conceptualized as a network, though not a network of objects or of individuals, but as a network of relations" (Donati, 2011, 226). Crossley (2011) suggests that, while conventional (sociological) analyses focus on individuals or societal "wholes," the most appropriate unit of analysis is instead social relations.

If we understand policy to emerge from interactions (i.e., relationships) among a network of policy actors, then policy analysis should be better able to account for the relational in explaining how and why policies work in the world. In Section 2, we conceptualize relationality and then discuss the implications of such conceptualizations for how we analyze policy.

As we will see in the empirical case study taken up later in this Element, a closer analysis of relationships gives us an understanding of how and why a new policy did not lead to expected outcomes in richer ways that, as seen in this case, can lead to fresh ideas for policy reform.

## 1.2 Goals of This Element

The goals of this Element are to

- provide a rudimentary definition of relationality in public policy,
- describe examples of how relationality is manifested in real policy situations,
- offer some initial ideas of how relational policy analysis can be done, and
- discuss how the relational lens can help us craft new ideas for policy reform.

We will use a case study to illustrate how a relational approach to analysis can be conducted, and how this leads to fresh insights into policy reform.

## 1.3 Relationality in Practice

Sometimes policy outcomes differ from that intended when the rationale for the policy, as designed, does not match those that motivate policy actors in the field. What is the logic of appropriateness that governs the decisions and actions of the actor in the field? Pierre Bourdieu (1977) probes into this complexity in his work on logics of practice (i.e., how patterns of action and reasoning at the field level may differ from that conceptualized by an external observer or an authority). His account of practice highlights the governing influence of relationships (e.g., dyadic relationships) on institutions.

Bourdieu, writing about things remote from public policy, gives a vivid description of how relational mechanisms work, using the example of gift exchange among the Kabyle of Morocco (Bourdieu, 1977). Gift giving among the Kabyle is a refined institution. It can never be a simple tit-for-tat exchange because that would make the interaction seem perfunctory. Rather than an objectively fixed obedience to social rules, the gift exchange has to operate as if it were spontaneous and improvised.

> "If it is not to constitute an insult, the counter-gift must be deferred and different . . . opposed on the one hand to swapping, which . . . telescopes gift and counter-gift to the same instant, and on the other hand, to lending, in which the return of the loan is explicitly guaranteed by a juridical act and is thus already accomplished at the very moment of the drawing up of a contract" (Bourdieu, 1977, 5).

Gift giving is more art than science, something that expresses a finely working relationship between parties. The gifts cannot be identical or even equivalent, since that would suggest the two parties were identical. It may differ between two peers or an elder and junior, for example, between two longtime friends and two chance acquaintances, between persons who share an interest in food and those who cherish books. Actors exchanging gifts must show care for the relationship.

The analogy to policy is that, just as with gift exchange, sometimes a policy is enacted in a way that cannot be prespecified or codified into a set of rules. The actual outcome is something inherently dependent on context, who the parties are, and what their relationship was, is, and will be. It is a particularly apt analogy for policy situations where:

- notwithstanding a codified or formalized set of rules or procedures that constitute a policy, its actual implementation, or embodiment varies from context to context in a way not captured by the formal policy;
- the formalized policy acts as a guide to policy action, but does not well circumscribe the action, as the latter is of a complexity that cannot be even approximately codified in a policy text;
- sometimes the formal policy acts as a facade, disguising the actual policy process that actors cannot acknowledge in any formal way.

If the last point seems extreme, note that such situations are more commonplace than one might think. For example, in 1964, California formally ended its bracero program, which had allowed the transient entry across the border of temporary farmworkers from Mexico. But the movement of migrant workers continued beyond 1964 despite never being sanctioned by official policy (González and Loza, 2016). In part, this was due to the continuing relationship between growers in Southern California and willing farmworkers in Mexico. In every context, we should be able to find examples of policies that work in ways not reflected in the official text.

Sometimes policy is crafted on a level that is (purposely or not) general, abstract, or ambiguous, and policy actors then have to translate this into working policies on the ground (Brugnach and Ingram, 2012). This situation, which might be likened to interpretation of a policy text, inherently brings into play relationships found in context. We may end up with a situation where policy is not isomorphic (i.e., not simply diffused) but polymorphic in that it varies from context to context (Lejano and Shankar, 2013). Current ideas about policy design are amenable to policy as something malleable, framed, and reframed by a network of policy actors continuously (e.g., Peters et al., 2018). The essential quality of a realistic, adaptable policy prescription process is that of openness (Dryzek and Ripley, 1988). Relationality is a lens for understanding how and why policy translation occurs (e.g., Alta and Mukhtarov, 2022). As Warne Peters and Mulligan suggest, problem-solving in the field is relational work (Warne Peters and Mulligan, 2019).

Admittedly, sometimes policy really does work in anomalous and divergent ways (e.g., Carter et al., 20154). But, we suggest, more often, the life of policy inherently proceeds nonanomalously in accordance with, and supported by, the relationships that are maintained among policy actors. A pattern of public action becomes an institution because it reflects and is supported by the everyday relationships found in that context. Take the simple example of an informal street vendor selling oranges on the corner. If this activity is maintained day in and day out, then we can say that it has become an institution. But to be an institution, it has to be supported by a web of relationships that actively maintain it – relationships between the vendor and orange-buying commuters and pedestrians, with officers who choose not to enforce vending permit ordinances, with building owners in that area, and so on. A relational approach seeks to make plain, and subject to analysis, the way relationships influence and even determine policy. One way to deal with this is to acknowledge that, yes, of course, relationships always matter, and leave it at that. The more interesting way is to explicitly analyze it and explain how.

In subsequent sections, we will be more explicit about what relationality is. This will require that we also attempt to be more analytical about just what a relationship is and how we might analyze it. We cannot hope to completely formalize the idea of relationship, since this broad concept defies definition. Relationships need not be dyadic, since they can inhere between many people or groups of people. Interpersonal relationships are never just individual-to-individual ones, and their meaning often goes beyond the immediate interaction (Bourdieu, 1977, 81). These can be multi-scalar, as relationships can inhere between persons, organizations, and institutions. They most often go beyond the material, as one can have a relationship with a cause or a concept (consider the idea of love for one's country). But we need ways to operationalize the idea of relationship to a degree that promotes policy analysis.

## 2 Conceptualizing Relationality

Policymaking is often portrayed as a rational activity – that is, a deliberate fashioning of policy to best achieve predetermined ends. The exercise is all the more rational to the extent that such fashioning of policy is done in a way that reasonably optimizes the chance of a policy's success. Understood in this way, policy is seen as ostensibly purposive; a prescription for achieving public goals.

In the discussion that follows, we set aside the complexity of policy for a moment and (artificially) draw a distinction between a rational model of policy and a relational one. This artificial, and somewhat playful, juxtaposing is pedagogical as, at some point, we return to the real world of policy where there are no clear-cut models, only the things themselves. The rational ideal is not the alpha and omega of policy thought as early writers might have once proposed, nor need it be the anathema of collective engagement that critics might charge; it is but one of many modes of description, all of them partial and incomplete. What it is, is a way of describing what policymakers and practitioners often aspire for and direct their activities toward – but it is not the only way. In our use of the word, rationality, we do not refer to the narrow idea of reason as instrumental/purposive (or the narrower idea of it as utility maximization) but the broader idea of applying the best of our knowledge, abilities, and multiple disciplines toward prescribing solutions to the problems of society, which is what Lasswell meant by introducing the idea of a policy science (Lasswell, 1970).

The most dominant notion of what rationality is, is conjured by the Cartesian ego, the autonomous individual (or subject) pondering the external world (or object) and divining what is true and good. The rational model is closely related to the idea of analysis, which has its roots in the Greek word, ἀνάλυσις, for taking something apart and inspecting it. The radical movement, applied to the field of policy analysis, involves, first, the separation of the analyst from the object of study and, secondly, the objective evaluation of the state of the object and the right course of action regarding it. In program evaluation, this takes the form of taking a policy or program in isolation, assessing its outcomes vis-à-vis intended objectives, and designing (or modifying) it to optimally meet those objectives. The subject, or analyst, is a person removed from the thing being studied, regarding it in objective fashion.

From this rational ideal comes the framing of policy as prescriptive. The rational decision-maker or decision-makers are those who, from their privileged perch, are able to apply criteria for what is true and good in judging something (say, a policy) as right or wrong and, if the latter, redesigning it for the better.

The idea of policy as *ratio* evokes the figure of the subject (or subjects) as that who is able to set explicit goals and prescriptions from a position external to a situation. These policies are then enacted, and their outcomes are assessed. The Cartesian subject sets policy from a position removed from the object of intervention (these objects invariably involve complex networks, including the public, field agents, organizations, and others). This is not an entirely radical model – in fact, rulemaking is idealized as done by external agents (e.g., legislators) viewing the situation from a more objective perspective. Policy analysis is often framed within a rationalist (even decision analytic) perspective – as one handbook suggests, policy analysis consists of specifying "explicit goals, concrete alternatives, systematic comparison, and clear recommendation" (Weimer and Vining, 2017, 372).

Embedded in much of the literature previously discussed is the implicit assumption of the policy actor as autonomous agent and, going further, rational decision-maker. It is in this light that we understand models of policy actors as employing individual rationality or, more pragmatically, bounded rationality involving coping strategies. But there is, by now, substantial literature on the psychology of identity and more complex models of decision-making, which speak to the person as a relational being, motivated to think and act in ways that cohere with one's relationships with others. We take a brief look at these bodies of thought, which support the relational perspective.

The early phenomenologists (Husserl, 1900/1901; Brentano, 1874) critiqued the Cartesian notion of *res cogitans*, the individual taking in the world and making judgments about it from an objective perch. Instead, they saw the person as defined by intentionality, or as a being always tending toward the other (e.g. Husserl, 1900/1901). Every mental activity, as Brentano would suggest, is something relational (1874). The person is never the external subject removed from the object being examined but, instead, someone embedded, from beginning to end, in the situation itself.

Later scholars would further the critique of the rationalist model. In moral philosophy, Gilligan began describing a model of human reasoning that was relational, more complex and contextual than the deontological laws of the rational ego (Gilligan, 1982). Instead of *cogito ergo sum*, the relational position might be better stated as *curae ergo sum* (we care, we form relationships, therefore we are). We understand who we are not autonomously but through our relationships with others. This is supported by social psychological research on identity, which promotes the idea that self is a multidimensional construct that goes beyond the individual. Brewer and Gardner describe how self-identity is constructed in three fundamental ways, which are self as the individual, self in dyadic relationships with others, and self as part of a group (Brewer and Gardner, 1996). This is important because the person shapes her actions in ways consistent with not just who she is as an individual, but with her relationship with others, and her membership in groups. In fact, the latter two dimensions of selfhood can both be included in what we refer to as the relational, as we are open to relationships that are not just dyadic. Relevant to this is parallel work on the inclusion of the other in the self (Aron et al., 1991).

People decide and act in ways that are guided by their relationships with others. We see this very directly in research on experimental games, where outcomes consistent with individual rationality are consistently deviated from. For example, in games of giving (e.g., dictator and ultimatum games), participants consistently give much beyond that predicted by individual rationality (e. g., Camerer and Thaler, 1995; Bolton and Ockenfels, 2000), in amounts often related to one's degree of social connection (or social distance) to the other (Bohnet and Frey, 1999). This is entirely consistent with the social psychology literature that suggests that, when one enters into a relationship, not only does one's self-conception include the other, but that decision-making becomes more altruistic toward the other as well (e.g., Cialdini et al., 1997). The idea that relationality matters in public policy owes much to insights from research in the areas of social psychology and experimental games that demonstrate how a person's decisions and actions are influenced by one's relationship with the other. This should hold true for policy actors at all points in the policy process, including those in the field who perhaps have face-to-face interactions with beneficiaries of policy.

We might take this as an alternative ontology of policy. In this formulation, policy is not the expression of the rational fashioning of rules and processes (by external decision-makers) to optimally achieve desired ends. Instead, we can view it as the working out of relationships among policy actors and, in this mode of description, policy emerges less as a rational fitting of means to an end, but as an expression of and coherence with the constellation of relationships among actors.

Policy then emerges in a way reflecting the active formation and maintenance of relationships. Having said this, policy is of course neither rational or relational – it is not captured neatly by any model; it is the thing in itself and is described by all these models in concert, and only partly so. The second caveat we make, before we proceed, is that should we take the relational route, analyzing policy in this manner might prove (as we will soon figure out) to be more complex than conventional approaches.

We previously provided a working definition of relationality in policy. There might appear to be some circularity to this because the definition rests on the idea of relationship, which we have yet to define. We will craft a working definition of it, with an eye toward its use for policy analysis, without suggesting that our working concept encompasses the expansive territory mapped by the word, relationship. If the goal is to better understand how policies evolve and operate in ways influenced by relationships among policy actors, then it would be useful to better conceptualize relationship in ways amenable to analysis.

There is an inextricable connection between identity and relationship. How we act with regard to another has very much to do with who we are, and who the other is. The other side of this connection is that who we are is, at least in part, defined by our relationship with others. As proposed in previous work (Lejano, 2008, 2021), relationship might be understood as the aggregate constitution of identity along three different axes, as shown below.

The Substance of Relationship
- constitution or expression of one's self-identity
- constitution or expression of identity vis-à-vis the other
- constitution or expression of identity of self-and-other

We propose that an adequate definition of relationship requires recognition of these different aspects of identity. Relationship with another, in other words, is defined by who I am, who I am in contrast or with regard to the other, and who I am conjoint with the other. Of course, there are other ways of understanding relationship, but the concept as defined above will suit our purpose of illustrating the merits of the relational view. It should be understood that this definition is most applicable in a local sense, that is, the entire aspect of one's identity is not necessarily brought into the encounter with another, but only those salient aspects that are relevant to or triggered by the situation at hand.

This formulation is also something that is limited to dyadic relationships among two individuals. The other can be a group, a society, an ideal, etc.

In some cases, the most pertinent dimension is a person's social identity, which pertains to being part of a group (e.g., Hornung et al., 2019).

This formulation helps us unpack the logic of "appropriateness" inherent in relational mechanisms. Policy can be directed (or redirected) in accordance with the web of relationships in which policy actors are embedded in. But what is appropriate or in accordance with such relationships? It is, simply put, what policy meanings and actions maintain existing relationships or even foster even deeper or more positive relationships. This is most obviously evident in the arena of political foes and allies, where an autocratic leader might direct public projects away from the former and toward the latter. These patterns, further- more, are inherent in identity – who these persons (or groups) are, who they are vis-à-vis the others, and who they are jointly. Such perverse behavior is part of the identity of the autocrat, and the autocrat's response toward the other depends on their relationship as allies or foes. Such patterns are obvious in glaringly perverse political situations such as autocracies. But here is an important point: these relational patterns are to be found in much more subtle forms among healthily functioning polities. If we look closely enough, we should be able to find these patterns at work in every political situation.

We have to delimit the notion of what constitutes relationality for the purposes of what and how we analyze while allowing its broader meaning to remain fluid and open. In the above discussion, we typify the relational as a dyadic relationship between two actors, but this is just the most convenient form for us to continue this particular exposition. The relational is neither bound by the dyadic, nor even the idea of linkages between individuals. It need not be envisioned as networks of ties, but in many other possible ways, such as fields within which different actors circulate and differently position (Bourdieu, 1984), assemblages of ontologically heterogeneous actants (Latour, 1993), narrative emplotments (Ricoeur, 1988), social-ecological systems (Bronfenbrenner, 1992), or multidimensional topolo- gies (Lejano, 2006).

The choice of how to frame the relational is not arbitrary. Grounding the rest of our discussion in the specific case of relationality as networks of social ties, let us turn to a specific illustration of the relational dimensions of policy.

## 2.1 A COVID Example

Consider a situation where there has been instituted a national mandate for wearing face masks in public places. And consider a political setting where translating this broad mandate into actual functioning policy is up to the mayor of each municipality. There is broad discretion over to what extent face masks are required and promoted, or whether the mandate is followed at all. It depends on the mayor's relationship with the national government and its leader, of course. It can also depend on her relationship with her electorate, especially the unions and other organizations that supported her. And it depends on people's relationships with each other since face masks are not just meant to protect self, but to protect the other. And, so, what policy is enacted, in exact terms, in that municipality, can hinge on all of these relationships. It also depends on who the mayor is, in terms of her prevailing political ideologies, positions regarding public health measures – in short, her identity. If we wish to understand why, in this municipality, the mandate was aggressively enforced while, in the adjacent one, it was willfully opposed, it may be possible to explain it in the context of these relationships. And explanation can even be too strong a word, but at least we should be able to understand it more deeply. This, of course, can quickly become quite complex. It may require going beyond dyadic relationships and beyond the immediate, personal scale of these relationships. The relationships, themselves, are not static conditions but something that evolves over time, possibly being affected by the mask mandate itself.

Some years back, prior to the COVID-19 pandemic, one of the authors spent time at a university in Hong Kong. While there, he was intrigued by the fact that, almost every week, someone would come to the department wearing a face mask. He asked someone why she was wearing one and was told that she had a cold and did not want to spread it to others at work. This speaks to a person's relationships with those directly connected to her – the person's social network if you will. Flash forward to the start of the pandemic in 2020, and we see how such relational phenomena affect policy. Before Hong Kong's city government even instituted any policies on face masks and other risk reduction measures, the city's residents jumped into action and began masking up en masse, along with other self-imposed social distancing measures.[3] Compare this to the troubled fate of mask mandates in many US cities, where millions equated it to a violation of individual liberty.[4] This choice, between foregrounding the priorities of the connected ego versus the autonomous one, is a relational one. But it's also not a binary phenomenon, where one is either connected or not, as

---

[3] Leung (2020). Part of the questioning would also inquire into how a person's identity and thought were influenced by the experience, growing up, of the SARS epidemic of 2003. Despite its outstanding work on promoting mask wearing, contact tracing, and other measures, the one thing Hong Kong most neglected can be understood as a relational phenomenon as well – and this was not promoting vaccination among residents in senior care centers. It was precisely these residents who were most isolated and whose social and physical ties to the main were most lacking. As the omicron surge of March 2022 wore on, the majority of residents in care homes remained unvaccinated (https://hongkongfp.com/2022/03/12/elderly-care-homes-in-eye-of-hong-kongs-deadly-covid-storm/).

[4] McKelvey (2020).

might be shown on a social network diagram. We are all relational beings, suspended in webs of meaning.

Were we trying to more thoroughly describe the mask-wearing colleague's response in relational terms, an interview might proceed with something like as follows. One could ask a series of questions. How would you characterize yourself as a member of this society, and how do you regard public health mandates? What is your relationship to those around you, such as at work, and how does this affect your reaction to the mandate? And, in addition, what is your relationship to the city as a whole, and what are your communities? In other words, one could explore the three dimensions described above, to begin analyzing the situation in relational terms.

Doubtless, these phenomena can be explained in other ways. For example, one can view the variation in mask mandates from locality to locality in the United States as the outcome of pluralist politics at work. But it is not simply the constellation of interest groups found in each place but the particular personal history, affiliation, and closeness each political actor has with these groups – in other words, the nature of the web of relationships. Indeed, just registering the presence of lobbies will not suffice, since one lobby may be present in two locales but will not have the same standing in these communities. To say that governance is a network phenomenon does not, for the same reasons, say enough, since similar-looking networks in two places may function quite differently, depending on the nature of the ties that bind the members together.

## 2.2 Convention and Anomaly

In this Element, we do not intend to completely circumscribe what relationality is, and what a relational approach to policy analysis consists of. We merely begin exploring the possibilities of using the idea of relationality to understand policy processes and their outcomes. What insights might emerge from foregrounding the relational? In some cases, we might find that a focus on relationality can help us discern how policy outcomes differ from situation to situation. In other cases, a relational approach can give us insight into how a broad policy mandate is translated into a more explicit, operational form in ways guided by the web of relationships found in the field. And a focus on the relational can help explain policy anomalies – when policies begin operating in ways other than intended.

Can relationality be used as a way to gauge or even measure different policy environments? Could we compare contexts according to the degree of relationality? Take, for example, how the Philippine political system is often referred to as one of "personalist" politics, meaning it is less about the rule of rules but about personas (or charisma, as Weber might put it). Politicians do not think twice about jumping parties and crossing over because party platforms are facile, ideologies are secondary, and what matters is that everything is transactional. This is an illustration of relationality. When, in 2017, the presidency went to Rodrigo Duterte, a ruthless advocate of military-style policing, the relationship between the executive, judiciary, and law enforcement agencies changed seemingly overnight. With the president encouraging the police to go beyond the law, what proceeded was an outbreak of so-called extra-judicial killings – the term, extra-judicial, signifying something "outside the law" (Pertierra, 2017).

In such a milieu, formal codified rules give way to the relational – no wonder that Philippine politicians constantly play with the idea of overhauling the constitution (a political dance that is referred to as the *cha-cha*, meaning charter change). In such a setting, codified rules are complemented (or supplanted) by informal transactions that take place behind the scenes – for example, traffic rules (and signs) can change from week to week, meaning drivers are prone to break a rule sometime, at which point, a traffic enforcer might suddenly appear, and transactions ensue. The everyday business of both public and private sectors are strongly relational – the logic of which is referred to as *palakasan* (or power play) which is, incidentally, the same word used for sports. And, when not coordinated, these alternative relational logics can offset the purpose of the rules – for example, one can see this in some Metro Manila streets where street lights are so closely spaced that their logic cannot just be based on illumination. Clearly, much can be explained using a relational lens.

So, is the relational frame of analysis something that is more applicable to some contexts than others –for example, neo-patrimonial states (Araral et al., 2019)? Without completely answering this question, we might venture a qualified "yes and no." Yes, in that some contexts feature more "anomaly" than others, which beg for a relational analysis to "the gap between *de jure* and de facto practices" (Bertelli et al., 2020, 742). But, no, in the sense that relationality should be seen as a feature of any policy environment, in any setting: Asia, the Americas, and Europe. Even the most formally rule-bound society carries out policy by coursing it through a network of policy actors. This is an important point: that the rule of law only works by the active working and reworking of relationships that maintain it. Regardless of which policy context we are examining, we should be able to employ the notion of relationality to understand it more deeply. But how we employ it can differ from context to context.

Anomalies notwithstanding, relationality should be important even when policy is crafted and delivered just as intended since, invariably, policy is coursed through a network of policy actors. Even the simplest change in a tax law requires coordination among many agents, including the internal revenue service, accountants, lawyers, and the taxpayers themselves. And the policy process is not simply analogous to the passing of a baton from one party to another, since each actor may be involved in interpreting, translating, and delivering the policy. We should find that the exact nature of the policy is finely influenced by the patterns and maintenance of relationships among these actors.

There are some types of policy situations where the relational dimension is particularly crucial, even in nonanomalous situations when the policy is carried out according to its formal intents. One such area might be that of conditional cash transfer (CCT) programs, where poverty alleviation or emergency assistance is carried out through direct outlays to recipients, usually in a means-tested manner and subject to some conditions (e.g., actively seeking employment, active attendance of children in public schools, etc.). In these programs, there is often a strong relational component that is needed, particularly in the interface with the potentially millions of recipient families. Identifying qualifying beneficiaries and working with them to explain and gain compliance with program conditions are tasks that can require extensive interface between policy actors. For example, in the Oportunidades-Prospera CCT program in Mexico, the nature of the direct relationships between frontline agency workers and beneficiaries were found to have a strong influence on the outcomes of the program, and beneficiary's availing of employment and health services improved with stronger relationships (Ramírez, 2021). In addition, the presence of *vocales*, or representatives elected by groups of beneficiaries, were found to be important relational agents who helped manage much of the interface between agency and beneficiary families (Fernandez de Castro and Lejano, 2018). CCT programs may be a type of policy situation that naturally introduces strong relational elements, often needing face-to-face interaction between program staff and recipients.[5]

Relationships mediate policy everywhere in every situation. Having made this sweeping statement, we might also speculate that some socio-political contexts are bound to exhibit greater relationality than others. In the implementation literature, there is considerable discussion of how street-level discretion is bound to increase in situations where the state has lesser capacities for governance (e.g., Grindle, 2017). The reasons include lesser abilities of the state to standardize policy implementation (through provision of resources, monitoring

---

[5] Networks of relationships need not consist of interpersonal contacts, as seen in Togo's NOVISSI program. This CCT scheme was done mostly digitally, where registered voters (and others, including non-voters identified through other means) simply used their cellphones to send a text, upon which their identities would be verified, resulting in an automatic transfer to the person's mobile money account (Debenedetti, 2021).

of agents in the field, etc.), lesser standards and processes for accountability, and more informality in policy implementation. Clientelism, which is a broad classification of what is essentially a relational phenomenon, is often associated with weaker governance systems (and younger, less developed democracies) in the developing world (notwithstanding the inherent orientalism in this view). Peake and Forsyth, in distinguishing between the Weberian, bureaucratic state and the informal, relational state, comment on how, in immature polities, the relational dominates governance (Peake and Forsyth, 2022).

In the following section, we trace some relevant bodies of scholarship in the literature, from public policy scholars and others, that support and supplement the incipient work on relationality.

## 3 Relational Accounts in the Literature

Scholars of public policy have long recognized the relational as a key element in policy processes. Early on, Lasswell noted how codified policies reflect and emerge from the workings of power relationships in society (Lasswell, 1958). "Power is always constituted and exerted in social relationships," write Arts and Tatenhove (2004, 350), describing agents-in-interaction in the policy process (see also Hoffman, 2013). Power is embedded in discourse, as we learn from Foucault (1975), which for some scholars also implicates the relational through "the socially constructed work of creating policy meanings and frames" (Healey, 2006, 14).

We do not suggest that the policy literature has ignored the crucial role of relationships. There have been earlier calls for a better rendering of policy and institutions in relational terms:

> "Rather than a macroscopic focus on system structure or a microscopic focus on the individual actor, we choose to build our model by focusing on what goes on in the social 'space' between actors ... What makes the institutions function is not the setting of clear lines of authority or individual interest, but the coherence of actions with the web of relationships" (Lejano, 2006, 233).

However, there has yet, to date, not been a concerted effort at foregrounding the relational aspects of policy in a systematic manner (Unwin, 2018). If relationships indeed are so central to the workings of policy, then perhaps it is time to subject it to serious analysis. How should scholars define a relationship, systematically categorize relationships, and perhaps even model them? How can a knowledge of the relational help explain policy processes and outcomes?

Policy scholars have long observed how the actual processes and outcomes do not match the formal prescription (e.g., Mazmanian and Sabatier, 1981; Pressman and Wildavsky, 1984; O'Toole, 2000). At times, divergent outcomes emerge from the decisions and actions of street-level bureaucrats (e.g., Lipsky, 1980; Frisch-Aviram et al., 2018). The essential phenomenon being described is that the logic behind the rules and prescriptions of policy, as espoused by a set of policymakers, are sometimes supplemented, or displaced by other logics, some of which we attribute to the relational. Even when enaction fully adheres to formal policy, it can do so in a way that elaborates on policy and fits it to more complex realities in the field – and, we suggest, part of the logic or ethic that guides such elaboration can be traced to the relationships that govern interactions in the field.

Oftentimes, codified policy is interpreted, modified, or elaborated on as it courses its way through a network of policy actors. But what determines how the policy evolves as it weaves its way through the network? There are many factors that can shape policy in the field, but foremost among these is the working and reworking of relationships among the policy actors. It is in the transactions among these actors that policy is translated into action. A number of things can foster this condition. Sometimes, rules are underspecified, allowing room for interpretation. Policy can reflect a particular form of underspecification, where policymakers do not fully specify policy as to allow implementers to tailor it to differing contexts (Clark et al., 2006). At times, this is reflected in a degree of policy ambiguity (Brugnach and Ingram, 2012), which can result from differences in how a heterogeneous network of actors interprets policy. Sometimes, policy can be misspecified, disguising illicit policies with formally acceptable policy text. Misspecification is what Lejano and Shankar (2013) refer to as policy double-talk, where the formal veneer of policy is presented on the frontstage while the real policy is crafted behind the scenes (Goffman, 1959). In more extreme cases, formalized rules and roles may become epiphenomenal to the working and reworking of relationships.

As an aside, foregrounding the relational provides even more justification for blurring the distinctions between policy design and policy implementation – after all, policy might be understood as what Barthes (1974) referred to as a "writerly" text.

One can understand the vagaries of policy as reflecting the complex nature of practice, which can be likened to an orchestra without a conductor (e.g., Bourdieu, 1977). Theorizing about the logic of practice, Bourdieu describes social structures that guide human behavior in tacit ways, embedded in the social milieu – what he refers to as habitus (Bourdieu, 1977). These unseen "structuring structures" ultimately are relational phenomena, which lie in the background but manifest themselves in the everyday life of a place. Policy actors operate within such habitus, their actions influenced in ways, seen and unseen, influenced by the webs of meaning in which they are enmeshed.

For example, Akram (2018) uses the concept of the habitus to trace the historical underrepresentation of women in the Australian Public Service.

Subsequent scholars of practice, in the areas of public policy and public administration, emphasize the embodied, emergent, nature of institutions that come about through the interactions of actors in their context (e.g., Colebatch, 2006; Bevir and Rhodes, 2010).

Attention to the relational is evident in the considerable literature on the role of social networks and policy networks in governance. Mostly, however, relationships in public policy contexts are analyzed structurally, examining their existence (as a binary variable) and other properties such as centrality and density (e.g., Arnold et al., 2017). Some researchers probe deeper into interactions and knowledge exchange between actors but, even with these, the main focus is on structural patterns of network ties (e.g., Crona and Bodin, 2006). What is lacking is a closer description of these relationships, the interactions that emerge from them, and their role in the trajectory and outcomes of policy.

The question of how we can describe and analyze the relational is an issue that remains to be fully worked out. In the social network literature, "links" between network actors are often characterized by simple binary ties between actors (i.e., linked, not linked), categorical associations between actors (e.g., friend, relative, neighbor) or by transactions (such as material, financial, etc.) that occur between them (Bodin and Crona, 2009). What we seldom find is any analytical attempt to more completely describe (especially in narrative terms) the complex, everyday nature of these social ties. A relationship, after all, is much more than a switch that one can describe as a zero-one variable.

More so than is found in the policy literature, public administration scholars have begun discussing varying notions of relationality and their implications for governance. Stout and Love discuss how governance is constituted by micro-level relational processes, such as face-to-face encounters among policy actors: " . . . in many ways, macrolevel governance is shaped by micro-level encounters in a scaffolding process" (Stout and Love, 2017, 130). Framed in this way, the relational perspective sees governance as emergent and co-determinative. This reflects earlier attention to "an appreciation of the ongoing production of organizational and material life through a network of interdependent human transactions" (Huising and Silbey, 2011, 15–16). Researchers in management and organization have begun studying how formal contracts and nonformalized, relational agreements interact (e.g., Poppo and Zenger, 2002; Bertelli and Smith, 2009). To quote Stout and Love, the relational is "a synthesis between embedded and independent social condition through the quality of relationality – a concept that acknowledges we exist within interconnected webs in which all entities (humans, nonhumans, physical objects, and places) co-determine one another" (Stout and Love, 2018, 70).

Bartels and Turnbull describe relational analysis as "an analytical focus on networks of interactions and relationships; explanation of the emergent properties that characterize their processes and outcomes of co-creation; and methodological foregrounding of social networks and their temporal and performative qualities" (Bartels and Turnbull, 2019, 6). The idea of governance as emergent has been a longstanding theme in this literature (e.g., Emirbayer, 1997; Crossley, 2011). This brings us back to the question: if policy and the institutions of governance are co-created and emergent, what logics guide these emergent properties?

At times, the emergent means an alternative system of rules and practices arising in contradiction to the codified rules. One way to depict this might be Goffman's analogy of processes occurring backstage versus front stage (Goffman, 1959). Stewart and Ayres (2001) discuss how policies sometimes act as general directives within which policy is worked out processually. Yet another would be to depict these as parallel, formal, and informal systems (e.g., Christiansen et al., 2004). But such depictions stop short of attempting to better characterize the generative forces behind the backstage and the informal, foremost among which are the working and reworking of relationships among policy actors.

In the broad area of institutional design, there are lines of work where the relational dimension is cast into the foreground more clearly. Scholars of regulatory design have begun focusing on situations where patterns of behavior do not conform to regulations per se, but instead emerge from everyday interactions among institutional actors (e.g., Huising and Silbey, 2011; Braithwaite, 2013; Warne Peters and Mulligan, 2019). This reflects an earlier focus on "rules-as-practiced," which involve allowing leeway for governed to tailor institutional practices to the particulars of its context (Ayres and Braithwaite, 1995; Gunningham et al., 1998). Stewart and Ayres describe how sometimes the output of rulemaking is procedural rather than substantive, a relational program within which policy is worked out processually within general directives (Stewart and Ayres, 2001; Braithwaite, 2013). Huising and Silbey use the term, "relational regulation," to describe how agents "govern the gap between regulatory expectations and performances with an appreciation of the ongoing production of organizational and material life through human transactions" (2011, 17). We ask: What process or logic substitutes for rule-governed behavior, in these situations? Simply stated, it is the logic of relationship – the steering mechanism provided by the working and reworking of interpersonal (and intergroup) relationships among policy actors.

A related development is that of "relational contracting" (Bertelli and Smith, 2010). Because of the difficulty of completely specifying the scope and detail of all these contracts, sometimes service providers and clients simply form a working relationship and work out the details within these relationships. As Bertelli and Smith describe this mode of contracting, "relationships enhance and expand the arrangements specified in a formal contract" such that "relationships have become the conduit for governance" (Bertelli and Smith, 2010, 22). Sometimes, contracting arrangements combine contractual and relational elements (Warsen et al., 2019). In the public administration literature, the term, relational governance, is used to refer to interorganizational transactions (e.g., purchasing of supplies or services) where relationships, supported by mutual trust, govern these exchanges rather than formal contracts. As Poppo and Zenger describe: "For such relationally-governed exchanges, the enforcement of obligations, promises, and expectations occurs through social processes that promote norms of flexibility, solidarity, and information exchange" (2002, 710). Relationships can pose advantages over formal contracts, such as lower transaction costs or increased flexibility and adaptability to changing circumstances (Heide and John, 1992; Dyer and Singh, 1998). Moreover, this type of flexible contracting is most likely to promote trust among parties than formal contracts.

Returning to the policy literature, considerable scholarship has been devoted to explaining the motivating factors behind the decisions and actions of policy actors, particularly what binds them to collective action. Sabatier et al. attribute behavior to belief systems (Sabatier, 1988). Motivational factors have been described in linguistic/textual terms as well, from the literature on meta-narrative (Rein and Schön, 1991), discourse coalitions (Hajer, 1993), or mutually constitutive narrative-networks (Ingram et al., 2014). But these motivations, as the phenomenologists might say, do not exist in and of themselves but are always directed toward something or someone. Behind these systems of belief, narrative, or discourse, there lies a constellation of relationships that give them shape. Beliefs, discourse, and narratives – these are all shared primarily through relationships (beginning with interpersonal ones) within a social network. But these bodies of scholarship have paid insufficient attention to the webs of relationships within which these policy networks evolve.

There is ample justification found in these various strands of literature for a focused attention on the relational dimensions of policy life. One persistent gap in each of the strands of literature mentioned earlier is the absence of any concerted effort to describe relationships among policy actors in any sufficiently rich way, and then, to connect these to the enactment of policy. As Kenis and Schneider suggest, "analysis that also includes the relationships between the different actors in policy-making is more powerful for understanding and explaining policy outcomes than studies that only include actor attributes and institutions in their analysis" (Kenis and Schneider, 2019, 472). There, however, remains the continuing challenge of how to capture, describe, and analyze relationships among policy actors.

## 4 Analyzing Relationality: The Challenge of Description

As a phenomenon to be analyzed, relationality is, practically speaking, unbounded. To simplify the point for a moment, suppose one were conducting a rational choice analysis of each person's, in a network of twenty people, willingness-to-accept (or other measure) vis-à-vis the mask mandate. One would survey each person in the group and assess twenty such values. But what if we were trying to account for each person's relationship with every other person in the group (and, to complicate it even further, with every coalition in the group)? We would be trying to assess a bewildering number of relationships.[6]

And how would we assess the relational in a way that respected its complexity? Were we to employ the three-dimensional analysis (of the individual, relative, and collective self) suggested earlier through in-depth interviews, how much text would we generate? What book-length description would we generate were we to attempt to ask a person to give a full autobiographical account of self and one's relationship with another (Bruner, 2003)?

The point is that, to try and meaningfully analyze relationality, one has to delimit the analysis in reasonable ways. After all, the policy researcher does not have the luxury of the anthropologist who might spend a decade in the Tobriand islands studying its culture and institutions. Moreover, one would not want to interview a person about their relationships with every other policy actor, but just a representation of this network. For example, one might ask street-level agents about their relationships, either in general or with a representative other, with their clientele. It would be prudent to focus on aspects of a person's autobiographical account that were more relevant to the situation at hand.

A relational analysis need not go fully into examining interpersonal relationships. One can study representations of these or categorical relationships (e.g., the general relationship in one county between agricultural extension officers and farmers). There should be a spectrum (or a field) of possible modes of relational analysis, ranging from the parametric to the fully autobiographical/ ethnographic. One can further delimit analysis to summary representations of the relational – short-hand accounts of relationship, if you will. In fact, we can (and maybe we should) characterize social network analysis as one such mode

---

[6] To be precise, at least $2^{n}-n-1$ such relationships, but this is beside the point.

of relational analysis, where relationships are described in an abbreviated manner as simple ties. To the extent that social network analysis attempts to explain the processes behind, and outcomes of, policy as influenced by the pattern of relationships in the network – this is relational policy analysis. The degree of complexity with which one describes relationships will depend on the particular needs of the study.

Some relational phenomena may act like Bourdieu's "structuring structures" which steer behavior in tacit ways, such that the actor may not even recognize these at work (Bourdieu, 1977). This further underscores the importance of relational analysis. To take an example, we might reflect on Habermas' notion of an ideal speech situation that envisions deliberation through an agonistic process (Habermas, 1985). Such an idealized model can lose sight of embeddedness, where these processes are enacted in an already structured field of relationships (Bourdieu, 1986). In this field, many actors who do not possess the same cultural and social capital as the dominant groups become alienated from the process. A relational perspective can highlight these phenomena and allow us to understand positionality in the field. Otherwise, it is hard to interpret what we hear or do not hear in a participatory forum, as voice (and silence) are structured by the unseen web of relationships.

The task of analyzing the relational is made all the more challenging by the fact that much of what we are trying to get often occurs in the backstages (or the wings) of the policy arena. Many relational phenomena occur behind what much of the literature on the policy process focuses on. What comes immediately to the mind of the reader would be the backroom deals that go on behind the scenes.

Just because analysis is potentially unbounded does not mean that we should avoid accounting for the relational. Social network analysis is a potentially unbounded endeavor, which is why the literature mostly focuses on dyadic, Boolean ties. The truth is that these limitations are present in the other modes of analysis as well. For example, accounting for belief systems invariably requires decisions about how to delimit one's inquiry into beliefs. And we note that these different approaches toward explaining policy processes and outcomes are not mutually exclusive. A relational approach can add to the insights gained by extant analytics, and vice versa. But this is part of the challenge of description and underscores the need for different approaches to relational analysis.

## 4.1 The Role of Narrative in Relational Analysis

Consonant with the task of analyzing relational dimensions of policy is the perhaps more elemental one of first capturing the nature of relationships among policy actors. How do we analyze relationship, itself? In this Element, we cannot resolve what will remain an open question. But it will help to trace some natural ways of accessing the relational, particularly through narrative.

Can we gauge or measure relationship? There is a literature on weak versus strong ties, but these modifiers are more suggestive than analytical. Beyond the binary, there is not much on how one might evaluate relationship. Some scholars of social network analysis mention the need to better link process and structure (e.g., Bodin and Crona, 2009). But it is inherently problematic how one might characterize relationships. Just defining a strong tie versus a weak one, or even coming up with parameters to measure this – this is problematic maybe in ways related to parallel efforts to quantify social capital (e.g., see Rogers and Jarema, 2015). There is something inherently complex about relationship – for example, take any dyad in a policy situation (e.g., the relationship between two world leaders), and ask, is the relationship positive or negative in valence? Invariably, unless the relationship is something overwhelmingly affirming or destructive, the ties between policy actors are not simply to be categorized as good or bad. They are simply things unto themselves. The best we can do is to try and faithfully describe them.

Fidelity to the web of relationships found in a policy entails deliberate focus on the particularity and contingency of the complex motivations and circumstances that drive policy actions. Bevir and Rhodes propose that this begs an interpretive approach to analysis and, particularly in American scholarship, has increasingly employed narrative analysis (Bevir and Rhodes, 2022).

In a discussion of how one might go about analyzing the relational, the use of narrative as an analytic device is a natural strategy. There is something that connects relationship and narrative in a natural way. Ask someone to characterize their relationship with someone else, and they may start telling a story or recounting previous experiences, which are narrative descriptions.

The way we relate to another is inherently an expression of who we are – our identity. But it is also formative of identity, as Piaget suggested in his work on child development (Piaget, 1952). As we discussed in Section 2, one way to characterize relationship is in terms of identity (I, I vis-à-vis them, I-and-them). Characterizing identity, in turn, is something that is inherently a narrative act. Ricoeur maintained that our sense of self-identity is essentially a working narrative that one tells, over the span of one's life, in a way that makes the disparate events, things, and people fit into a coherent account – an action he called emplotment, which he defines in the following manner:

> "I shall broadly define the operation of emplotment as a synthesis ... between the events or incidents which are multiple ... that it organizes into an

intelligible whole. The plot, however, is also a synthesis from a second point of view: it organizes together components that are as heterogeneous as unintended circumstances, discoveries, those who perform actions and those who suffer them, chance or planned encounters, interactions between actors ranging from conflict to collaboration, means that are well or poorly adjusted to ends, and finally unintended results" (Ricoeur, 1991, 21).

This helps us understand the natural connection between relationship and narrative. One's interrelationship with another is fraught with interactions, encounters, and chance events, and the way one naturally makes sense of all that is through construction of a narrative.

For this reason, our attempts to faithfully describe relationships among policy actors may naturally lead to receiving and subsequently analyzing narrative accounts from the respondent. This is easily seen in the case study described in the previous section, where the research essentially consisted of having informants simply share their stories of what they experienced as they navigated the new voucher program. In sharing the experience, they invariably also share aspects of their identities and their relationships with other policy actors (family, professionals, peers). In fact, in our experience, the interview does not even need to frame in terms of identity and relationship – simply allow the informant enough time and space to tell a story, and they eventually start talking in autobiographical terms. And, if it is true that we are relational beings, then our autobiographic narratives invariably touch on relationships with others.

Narrative is also a natural vehicle for reforming power imbalances in governance. As Lyotard pointed out, while technical discourse is often the privileged language of those in power, it is narrative that is the language that binds community (Lyotard, 1984). Narrative can then be a way of giving voice to the most marginalized (Harris, 2021). Narrative can be a vehicle for revealing needed policy reforms and reconnecting those disenfranchised from the process (e.g., Huff and Cooke, 2022).

The narrative aspects of relationality provide a good contrast to the unidimensional representations of relationship, as found in social network analysis. While not something we can venture into in this Element, one wonders at the potential, if it were possible, for benefiting from the insights from both the systematic, calculable metrics of social network analysis and the rich description of narrative. To be clear, narrative is just one route to the study of the relational, but we feel that it will prove to be a primary vehicle for relational research.

## 4.2 An Illustration

How does one proceed to do relational analysis? This should be an important area of new research, moving forward. The systematic study of relationality is a new field of inquiry, and we are just beginning to sketch out what the possibilities are for analysis. We've suggested that social network analysis could be regarded as a type of relational work, and this is the area of analysis that has an extensive history and literature behind it. But analyzing relationality in richer ways and using these approaches to explain and analyze policy – this is largely unexplored.

At this early stage in the research, it makes sense to cast a wide net and be liberal about what a relational analysis is and what it does. We might begin with the notion that a relational analysis can be any type of study that examines how relationships among policy actors somehow influence policy. This is about as broad a definition that we can start with. Many examples fall within this orbit. For example, an analysis of how nongovernmental actors wove their influence in and out of state departments and the Pentagon, private contractors, and think tanks, and helped bring the United States to war with Iraq. Through their multiple and overlapping relationships with policy actors, these individuals constituted a "shadow government" that moved policy in ways unacknowledged by government (Wedel, 2009; also Craft, 2015). Such examples examine what occurs in the backstage of policy life, but relationality affects readily ostensible policy processes as well. A different type of shadow government is seen in the increasing role of voluntary organizations in the delivery of welfare and other services (Wolch, 1990). Trudeau (2008) discusses how relationships among these nonprofits and state agencies are highly contextual and how these relationships can steer the nature of service delivery.

In another example of policy analyses that foreground the relational is Wilshusen's research on the micropolitics of everyday transactions, which occur largely "off-stage," in determining the outcomes of a community forestry program in Quintana Roos, Mexico (Wilshusen, 2009). Carey et al. (2009) provide a case study of an Australian nonprofit supplementing the depersonalized professionalization of care for hep-C patients by creating community spaces that nurtured interpersonal relationships. Whether the relational processes occur away from the forefront of the formal policy process or within it, these are all examples of how attention to the relational can help us deepen our understanding of a policy situation.

To begin with, what are the goals of a relational analysis? While answering this is something that should emerge through more widespread use of relational approaches, there are some aspects that we can already point to at this time. An analysis might be guided by one of the objectives listed below (or several of them, or something altogether different from these).

Possible Goals of a Relational Analysis
- to show how a broad policy mandate gains specificity or contextuality as it is coursed through a network of policy actors
- to uncover how and why a policy functions in ways different from that formally codified
- to evaluate how some policies, programs, and institutions function through relational ties instead of formal rules, roles, and contracts
- to demonstrate the need for active, responsive, and functioning relationships across a network of policy actors, if policy is to be crafted and carried out effectively
- to explain how policy implementation depends on functioning relationships among a network of actors, and furthermore, to demonstrate how this creates differentiation across situations

The last point emphasizes the contextuality of policy. At times, we have a policy that, rather than applied in uniform fashion across the field of implementation, attains a kind of contextuality wherein it achieves fine differentiation from context to context. This has been elsewhere referred to as polymorphism, in contrast to the idea of isomorphism in the institutional literature (Lejano, 2006). The point is that what generates this kind of polymorphism is none other than the working or reworking of relationships in place, which would differ with context.

In the following discussion, we use an extended example to illustrate relational analysis, a sketch that suggests some of the potential uses of a relational approach, and the unique insights we can gain from it. This particular example involves extensive use of narrative (extracted from interview transcripts), which is one effective approach to relational analysis.

### 4.2.1 Vouchers for Social Service Delivery: An Extended Relational Analysis

The following example clearly illustrates how failing to recognize and include relational phenomena in the design of a policy can detract from the policy's effectiveness in practice. We take up a case study of a new policy instrument that was initiated, with varying results among the target population. We do so in order to illustrate how we might analyze the relational dimension of the policy and highlight the rich insights afforded by such an approach. The example is that of a new policy that utilizes vouchers for encouraging greater autonomy (of policy recipients) over social services for the aging population.

This case study is one that shows the relational dimension clearly (and, so, for illustration, serves our purposes well). The reason is that, as the analysis will show, the aspects of policy that seem to most influence whether the voucher is used or not are relational in nature. It is not so much in the formal rules of the voucher program that these issues come up but in the presence or absence of relational capital (i.e., relationships that each voucher client can draw from to make up for issues with mobility, literacy, and others).[7] It is only when we interview voucher clients that the crucial relational elements come to the fore, and we realize that changing the general, codified rules would not address these directly (especially since these issues are highly contextual).

In many contexts, the state subsidizes (and often, directly provides) a wide range of social services such as welfare, child care, health and nutrition, mental health, and others. Invariably, state-centered programs have to answer the central question: Are the right services being provided, in the right amounts, to the right people, in a reasonably cost-effective manner? Sometimes, this type of critical inquiry has led to what some might refer to as a neoliberal solution of privatizing service delivery, essentially letting the market decide. In other cases, the state retains its jurisdiction, but with the creation of quasi-market conditions where market forces inject its type of rationality into the programs. One example of the latter has been the use of vouchers for social services, which are designed to give service recipients more choice over the services they receive.

Its original proponent, Milton Friedman, suggested that the voucher is a policy instrument that provides each user freedom of choice by turning the public system into something like a market (Friedman, 1962). At its core is an efficiency argument, as this market-like arrangement would optimize the matching of supply and demand for services. It would also, at the same time, minimize transaction cost, as interactions between clients and government agencies would decrease, as the client would only need to choose from a menu of options. A key to the concept behind a voucher is that, as a policy instrument, it works autonomously and automatically – that is, by simply creating a flexible voucher, users and providers automatically adjust their choices and offerings, respectively, to optimize the matching of demand and supply. This has the potential to reduce the institutional apparatus and "red tape" associated with a program. And, by virtue of consumers' increased ability to decide for themselves their optimal suite of services or products, the voucher can work to increase the individual's autonomy and independence from the state.

---

[7] Rivera et al. (2021, 283) use the term, relational capital, to describe "the ability of an agent to positively interact with other agents, and it is characterized in terms of mutual commitment, mutual trust, and the strength of social ties."

In 2012, the Hong Kong government launched an initiative to improve aging services through the use of a means-tested voucher. In implementing the Community Care Service Voucher for the Elderly (CCSV), the Hong Kong government sought to strengthen community aged care and achieve the policy of aging-in-place through a more flexible and diverse service delivery model. The CCSV program gave older service users a voucher that they could use to directly select the service provider, the service type, and the service package that best fit their needs (Legislative Council Secretariat, 2012; Sau Po Centre on Ageing, 2015). The CCSV's core philosophy is a "money-follows-the-user" approach (Chui and Law, 2016), the rationale behind it being to increase the clientele's choice and flexibility in service utilization and, at the same time, promote the efficient, equitable, and effective use of public funds (Chui, 2011). The CCSV works on the supply side, as well, as it encourages new service providers to enter the market and, through competition, improves quality of service (Legislative Council Secretariat, 2012).

So, the key idea is the increasing autonomy of the service recipient and decreasing reliance on the government agency, which is supposed to intervene less in the day-to-day selection and management of services. Instead, decision-making is supposed to be diffused, centered around the individual, who assumes the role of an informed consumer. This echoes the vision of Milton Friedman (1962), who sought to give the service recipient greater agency and self-determination – in fact, aspiring to a market situation where the consumer has complete choice over which commodity to purchase, in such a manner, reducing the individual's reliance on agents of the state and creating a program that works autonomously and automatically with minimal involvement by government. In the health sector, the voucher is seen as an instrument for increasing the power of the service recipient and decreasing that of the provider (Ramesh et al., 2014).

The Hong Kong Government launched the first phase of CCSV as the pilot scheme in September 2013 to test the viability of new service delivery model in community care services. The CCSV pilot scheme was also extended into its second and third phases in October 2016 and October 2020 respectively. During the first phase of the CCSV pilot scheme, evaluators identified a major short-coming in the low utilization rate, more than 50 percent of those eligible refused the CCSV (Sau Po Centre on Ageing, 2015). However, after eight years, under-utilization remains a persistent problem (HKGSAR, 2021).

During the first phase of the CCSV program, one of the co-authors conducted an evaluation of process of voucher utilization, especially as experienced by the clients and their carers. Specifically, she wanted to understand what differentiated those cases where the service recipients successfully employed the voucher versus those where they could not. The analysis underscores a key insight advanced in this Element: that relationships mattered in ways not recognized, assessed, or provided for in the design of the policy.

Of particular interest in the subsequent discussion is how relational aspects were analyzed, and how the relational is linked to the effectiveness of the policy. And, lastly, how such analyses can be developed into recommendations for policy reform.

In this study, certain kinds of relational factors were identified as key (Kan, 2018; Kan and Chui, 2021). The study adopted a qualitative approach to examine views and experiences among voucher recipients, family caregivers, and professionals regarding the CCSV, posing the following research questions: (1) Why do some people use the CCSV and others do not? (2) What are the differences between CCSV users and CCSV nonusers in their stores of relational capital (a concept we will discuss below)? (3) How do family relationships, professional support, and peer interaction affect the utilization of the CCSV?

CCSV clients, family caregivers, and professionals were recruited through purposive sampling for individual in-depth interviews. This involved fifty-three interviews with CCSV clients and caregivers, which were composed of twenty-six within the CCSV users group (i.e., those who successfully utilized the voucher) and twenty-seven within the CCSV nonusers group (i.e., those who did not successfully utilize the voucher). Additionally, sixteen interviews were conducted with professionals, which included eight responsible social workers and eight service providers. All interviews were recorded and transcribed for thematic analysis.

A semi-structured in-depth interview, designed to solicit stakeholder narratives, was used to probe the thoughts and experiences of different stakeholders with the CCSV. Interviews ranged from forty-five minutes to ninety minutes in length with the researcher referring at intervals to an interview guide which covered the following areas: (1) perceptions and experiences on CCSV; (2) choice and decision-making in CCSV; (3) personal capacity; (4) family support and social network; and (5) institutional support. All interviews were recorded and transcribed for thematic analysis.

The findings of the study showed that relational factors, including family relationships, professional support, and peer interaction acted as facilitators of or barriers to the CCSV utilization. Table 1 provides a summary of the themes and occurrences of each theme within the interview transcripts.

The key finding: the main difference between CCSV users and CCSV nonusers in the service utilization was the presence or absence of supportive relationships. First, we note that those who are eligible to use the CCSV are those on the waitlist of subvented long-term care services, many of them dealing with various physical or cognitive conditions (e.g., mobility problems, dementia). For many of these voucher users, there are significant barriers to visiting different service units, comparing different service packages, and making the service decisions unassisted. Among the current cohort of voucher recipients, the study found large numbers of clients with challenges in terms of education and literacy – thus, many experienced difficulties accessing and digesting information about the new voucher service program and its related mechanism about service choice. But, importantly, even though some may experience these challenges, the study found that they still can participate in the decision-making process with the help of family members or professionals. In other words, the presence (or absence) of these relational factors proved to be "resources" that operated behind the scenes to support (or impede) the client's use of the voucher.

As reflected in Table 1, for all of the successful voucher users, there was the presence of at least one kind of relational support. The most significant

**Table 1** Relational themes and occurrences in interview transcripts

| | | Number of occurrences | |
| --- | --- | --- | --- |
| **Themes** | **Findings** | **CCSV Users**[*] | **CCSV Nonusers**[*] |
| Family relationships | Close and supportive family relationships – Relationships/Family (+) | 48 | 3 |
| | Lack of family support and involvement – Relationships/Family (−) | 2 | 25 |
| Professional support | Strong worker–client relationships – Relationships/Professionals (+) | 35 | 0 |
| | Lack of professional support – Relationship/Professionals (−) | 2 | 30 |
| Peer interaction | Encouragement from peers – Relationships/Peer (+) | 6 | 0 |
| | Lack of advice from peers – Relationship/Peer (−) | 0 | 2 |

(adapted from Kan and Chui, 2021).

[*] *Note.* Total number of CCSV users was twenty-six while total number of CCSV nonusers was twenty-seven.

relationship for facilitating the use of CCSV was a close and supportive family relationship, which refers to any kind of family support, such as the provision of information, emotional support, physical assistance, and financial resources that can assist older family members in understanding the CCSV program and making informed choices regarding the voucher utilization. The second important relational factor is professional support, which involves all the information, explanation, guidance, and direction provided by responsible social workers. The study demonstrates how strong worker–client relationships can empower clients to make informed choices with the CCSV. Furthermore, positive peer interaction and relationships are also a key relational factor, which includes all the information, shared insights, and encouragement provided by a peer group, which can encourage clients to try the CCSV program. Note that none of these relational "resources" are considered in the design of the voucher policy.

In the case of CCSV nonusers, almost all of them lacked support from family and professionals, and some of them mentioned the absence of a peer group. Another interesting finding was that the lack of certain kinds of relational support can be compensated by other forms of relationship. For example, the responsible social worker could assist those clients who had no children to assist them with the CCSV. Relationships can be seen as multiple and interacting forms of (social and other) capital, where one kind of capital can compensate for decrements in another.

KEY INSIGHT

Relationality is a key factor behind successful policy. The new voucher did not work in autonomous/automatic fashion (as might a market situation where consumers simply choose from an array of commodities). Rather, successful voucher users depended on a network of active relationships, and the presence and quality of relationships determined how well the policy worked. Since these relational aspects are not usually considered in crafting policy, policy actors are often left without sufficient "relational capital."

How was the analysis conducted? As we proposed in the previous section on analysis, we took a narrative approach, involving interviewing informants and encouraging them to tell their story regarding their experience with the new voucher program. And analysis of the text involved extracting themes and key insights from the interview transcripts. The relational dimensions of voucher utilization between users and nonusers will be illustrated by quotations in the next section. Most important, to readers of the Elements in Public Policy series, is to see how one type of relational policy analysis might be done. In this case, it requires close reading of the stories that policy actors share.

*4.2.2 Describing the Relational Dimensions of Voucher Use*

We now illustrate how the analysis of relationships (among different policy actors) helps us understand how and when the voucher succeeds and fails. How does a relational analysis help us explain those cases when the voucher was effectively used, and the cases when it was not?

· In the following section, we illustrate one mode of relational analysis, which accesses autobiographical narratives from informants regarding the experience of the policy situation; many of these passages also appear in one of the co-authors' previous work (Kan and Chui, 2021). In the interviews, conducted mostly in Cantonese, we note the frequent use of terms that describe various kinds of relationships, such as 關係 (*gwaan hai*, relationship), 聯繫 (*lyuen hai*, connection), and 感情 (*gam cing*, affection).

**Family Relationships**

The CCSV program being a novel pilot model for community aged care services in Hong Kong, most of the public (including potential voucher uses, family caregivers, and professionals) were unfamiliar with its new service content and service mechanism. Many eligible clients were dealing with some physical and/ or cognitive impairment. Level of educational attainment seemed to be a factor, as well. To overcome all these personal constraints, supportive family relation-ships emerged as a key factor in helping clients understand more about the voucher program and assisting them in making informed choices with regard the use of CCSV, as illustrated in the quotations below.

Ling [78, female, CCSV User]

> "My daughter visits the center with me and she says the service (CCSV) is good since she has already helped me read all the information about the voucher program and she also has helped me talk to the social worker in the center, and finally I made the decision to join its services…without the help from my daughter, I would not be able to visit the center by myself as I cannot walk well and I dare not take the bus alone. And also I did not receive any formal education [and] I don't understand the information written on the leaflet about the voucher program. I have one son and two daughters, and one daughter has a very close relationship with me. Although we are not living together, she helps me a lot in my daily living."

The daughter of Mandy [67, female, CCSV User]

> "My mom cannot walk so she seldom goes out, she just stays home all the time … the only activities for her are eating and sleeping at home. Without our help, I don't think my mom could use the service (CCSV) because she doesn't want to give herself and others trouble. Thus, she prefers staying

home...my three sisters and I are very concerned about our mom, [and] all of us have a very close relationship with her (my mom), thus, we picked two service units which are close to my mom's home from the brochure and then visited these two units by ourselves first to collect more information about the scheme (CCSV)...our family discussed service options with two officers in charge (service providers). Both were very professional, helpful, and friendly, and they explained their services to us clearly. After that we encouraged my mom to use the service. We accompanied her to the service units to make her feel safe and comfortable ... finally, we let my mom to make the decision by herself as she says she likes the service (CCSV) and the first service unit we visited ... now my mom uses the service, [and] she can connect with our community and make some friends in the center instead of staying home all the time."

As seen in these quotations, close family relationships offer CCSV participants different kinds of support, such as collecting a large amount of information and screening service providers. Families can also accompany them to visit different service units, giving them emotional support and encouraging their use of voucher services. In fact, family members can assist them during the decision-making process by supporting their capability to exercise their own choices and decisions, as heard in the quotations below.

Among CCSV nonusers, on the other hand, the absence of relationships, especially with supportive family members, hindered them from making informed choices vis-à-vis voucher services. Furthermore, as illustrated in the quotations below, the lack of both family and professional support were significant factors impeding CCSV utilization. The support networks of some older people who live alone can be very weak. In many cases, children live outside the city and are not able to provide them any support in the use of CCSV. These insights emerge from interviews, as seen in the quotations below.

Amy [79, female, CCSV Non-user]

"I am living alone. I have three few daughters but every time when I ask them for help, they just say that they are busy. I don't know what they are busy with. They seldom visit me, our relationship is not very close. I seldom go to the social centre for older people, I don't have any social workers follow my condition. I don't know them (the social workers) well ... I did not ask for any help or advices from them on this matter (CCSV), I don't want to bother others ... To make it simple, I just decided by myself not to use the voucher services."

Dai [female, social worker, service provider]

"I heard from an older person that he had received the voucher for 4 months, but he did not use the voucher service because he actually did not know how to choose the service provider because his responsible social worker only gave him the voucher without any explanation and follow-up actions. In addition, that older person's son is too busy to earn for a living, his son got no chance to help his father regarding the voucher services, and I heard that his son can just visit him two or three times a year and sometimes call him by phone, seems their relationship is not very close."

Wang [female, social worker]

"For my cases, all older people or elderly couples who are living alone without family support, they did not join the CCSV scheme because they don't know how to shop around different voucher service units if their family members don't have time to help them . . . just like one of my cases, Mrs. Chan, she is living with her husband, they have one son and one daughter, both of them get married and living very far away from Mr. and Mrs. Chan, their son is working and staying in China most of the time while their daughter has to take care of her own family and baby, so it is impossible for both their son and daughter to keep a very close contact with them . . . Mrs. Chan is suffering from dementia and her husband (Mr. Chan) is very old too, I have tried my best to explain the voucher services to them but they still cannot understand it well, I cannot contact their son as he is not in Hong Kong at the time, and their daughter is not able to help them too. Actually, it is quite exhausting or even impossible for Mrs. and Mr. Chan to visit all the voucher service units and then select the service by themselves."

Furthermore, without other forms of support, such as from social workers, some potential clients choose not to use the CCSV. This shows the importance of relationships with professionals, discussed next.

## Professional Support

The second important relational factor is the worker-client relationship, that is, professional support from (often) a responsible social worker. The interviews show how social workers play an important role in empowering clients to make informed choices to use the voucher. Furthermore, strong worker-client relationships can compensate for the lack of family relationships and afford informed choice and decision-making. For example, social workers can mobilize different community resources to assist them in the decision-making process.

Winnie [68, female, CCSV User]

"Mr. Chow (the social worker) told me that I am selected for the voucher scheme . . . he has arranged a meeting for all older people, including me, who have been invited for the voucher services and explained the scheme to us in very details including the service content, payment, the number of service days . . . he even tells us that we can change the service unit if we find that the services are not suitable for us . . . Mr. Chow is very helpful and has a very good relationship with me and other older people. He calls and visits me regularly, whenever I need help, I will find him too ... During the talk, many other social workers help the older people to fill the form and explain the service, especially for those older people who cannot read and write."

Peter [61, male, CCSV User]

"Mr. Li, the social worker is very helpful. He visits me and explains the voucher scheme to me in details as he knows that it is not convenient for me to go to his office. He gives me a booklet and a few pages of information about the CCSV program. He recommends 6 centres to me. I am single with no children, I find nobody to help me except Mr. Li ... my relationship with Mr. Li is very close, whenever I have problems, I will call him at once. Every time Mr. Li can help me ... just like this time after I have selected two centres for the voucher services, Mr. Li helps me to find a volunteer to accompany me to visit those two centres physically because I cannot walk well so it is impossible for to visit the centre alone ... "

On the other hand, without professional support from social workers, it is difficult for some clients, including some who have no formal education, to study the CCSV program and make informed choices, as illustrated in the quotation below.

Cheung, [87, male, CCSV Non-User]

"I did not join the scheme because I don't know what it is, actually. I did not receive any formal education, I cannot read the information, on the leaflet ... the responsible social worker did not explain the CCSV to me, I don't even remember the name of social worker, she just said all the services are suitable for me and asked me to choose the service by myself ... I never got married so I don't have any children to help me. I also don't want to bother others."

Son of Ng, [84, male, CCSV Non-User]

"I live with my father and my mother, so our relationship is very close ... recently, I have noticed that my father's health condition is becoming worse and worse ... I worry about him so much and I really want to find a good service which is suitable for him. However, I need someone to tell me what kind of services my father actually needs ... even though I have a university degree, I am not an expert in that area (elderly care services)...I have already told the social worker and the service unit staff, I cannot make the decision, because I don't know what is good for my father ... all of them just ask my father to join the service (CCSV), nobody can explain it to me in detail. I feel helpless actually. I feel that all these professionals are not so helpful."

Even for clients with family support and close family relationships, strong worker–client relationships are still an important relational factor in effective CCSV utilization, since social workers are professionally trained workers who can assess clients' needs and recommend suitable services for them. They are also seen as mediators who can help clients with other crucial relationships (e. g., with service providers). These insights led to recommendations to formalize social workers' role as individualized case managers (as will be discussed in the next section).

## Peer Interaction

The empowering effect of relationship extends to peer interaction. Positive recommendations and encouragement from a person's peer networks can facilitate them to make informed choices and decisions in the use of CCSV, as illustrated below.

Daughter of Anita [93, female, CCSV User]

> "In the very beginning, my mom's close friend says this centre is very good and asks me to apply for the voucher services for my mom. My mom's friend is very helpful, she even gives me the booklet about the voucher scheme . . . after reading the booklet, I approach the social worker who follows my mom's long-term care, to ask about the details of the voucher scheme. Our relationship with that social worker is very close, she always calls me to check with my mom's health condition. This time, the social worker can also explain the voucher programme to me in details . . . finally, I accompany my mom to visit this centre, without my assistant, my mom cannot go alone as she is using walking frame . . . after visiting the centre, I believe this centre can provide professional training to my mom and improve her mobility, the staff here in the centre is very friendly and professional."

---

These accounts point to the central role played by a client's web of relationships in utilizing the new voucher. Contrary to how vouchers are conceptualized, they do not act in autonomous fashion, automatically creating a market-like situation where consumers freely choose from a set of providers. Instead, the effectiveness of the voucher program depends on the client's ability to access and manage different forms of social and cultural capital, especially in the form of interpersonal relationship.

The preceding example was illustrative for several reasons. First, it provides an example of how even the simplest kind of relational diagnostic, the presence or absence of relational ties, helps us understand policy success. But it goes beyond this – after all, simply registering the presence or absence of ties is something that a conventional social network analysis could do, as well. Second, the example illustrates the degree of empiricism (in this case, involving the close reading of narrative text) that may be required for relational analysis. We enter into the nature of ties among policy actors, and we use interviews to reveal how different types of relationships function to allow the policy to function properly. These interviews describe the nature of the relationships, and informants use different terms to describe the properties and valence of each relationship. We hear, in the interviews, about mechanisms by which different forms of relational resources work to compensate for other lacking resources (e.g., decrements in the client's financial or cognitive health). But listening to people's accounts does not simply lead to idiosyncratic stories about relationships – rather, we find relational patterns that are useful for improving policy. We find overlapping relational phenomena that recur, which can lead to institutional reform.

KEY INSIGHT

Relationships can be seen, and utilized, as resources that institutions can deliberately employ and enhance. The social construction of various policy actors, including the traditional beneficiaries of a policy, can sometimes essentialize these in ways that policymakers oversimplify. Instead, we should see these actors as agents embedded in their respective relational milieu. Policymakers should take into account how different actors have access to varying forms of such relational capital and incorporate this into policy. Relational capital is part of the "inner workings" of policy, however, which means that they are often overlooked in formal policymaking.

It is clear that informed choice does not comport with any simple model of individual decision-making but, rather, something that happens within a network of connected individuals and groups (also see Millar et al., 2019). And the relational approach helps policymakers not view targets of policy in essentializing ways, as if persons dealing with cognitive or physical difficulties are automatically incapable of self-determination (Dobson, 2015). Rather, their capabilities are, at least to some extent, embedded in the relational milieu they inhabit.

What did we learn from analyzing policy from a relational perspective? In the case of the CCSV program, it is clear that closer (and formal) attention to relationships is needed to increase voucher utilization. The fact that the relational dimension is neglected in formal policymaking creates gaps in the effectiveness of the policy. To put it another way, the working and reworking of relationships have a strong determinative effect on what the policy is for program recipients and professionals in the field. The analysis also shows how relationships might be thought of as a kind of capital, what some scholars refer to as *relational capital* (Capello and Faggian, 2005; Johnston and Lane, 2018) which can be regarded as resources or mechanisms for enacting policy. This leads to recommendations for reforming policy that should be, at least in some respects, relational in nature. We take up the latter idea next.

## 5 Implications for Policy Reform

The previous discussion on relational analysis has been relatively non-normative in tone. The key idea in analysis is mainly about tracing how relational phenomena affect policy. Less has been said about normative considerations – that is, whether the suite or relationships are good or bad, or whether it is good or bad that policy might turn so much on the reach and nature of these relationships. But one can only forestall the normative consideration for so long. After all, many situations, where relationships strongly influence the outcomes of policy, are identified with corruption. We demarcate bureaucracies between those that are thought to be professional from those that are more "transactional." But, to put a mild suggestion, there are times perhaps when one can employ a weak form of epoché, where one first describes the thing as it is (i.e., relational phenomena) as faithfully as possible, and only then apply a normative lens.

First, the concept of relationality is not good or bad, in and of itself. The nature of relational arrangements found in a policy situation can be necessary or detrimental to effective policy. Many of the most hopeful suggestions for enlivening policy situations involve improved relationships with an engaged public, more collaborative arrangements, and closer interactions between government and governed. In some cases, there are calls for co-determination (or co-design), where those most affected by policies have a greater hand in their construction. These are usually presumed to be good directions for reform (whether they actually prove successful is another matter). And these all speak to necessarily relational aspects of policy.

In this section, we turn our view to the possibility of viewing the connection from a different direction and thinking about policy reform. Improving public policy may require explicit attention to relational elements, such as relationship-building among the polity, sustaining existing relationships, and reforming broken ones. For example, what is the call for more collaborative governance if not a call for improving relationships between decision-makers and the governed? In doing so, however, it is not enough to simply do so in a categorical way, as if there were a universal template for collaborative governance – instead, it must be realized in context, within the particulars of social networks involved in the policy situation.

If, as we argued in previous sections, the richness of policy life is seen in the working and reworking of relationships among policy actors, then calls for policy reform must somehow involve reforming the relationships that undergird policy. Relationships are not static, even if embedded in the habitus of society. They evolve, they break, and they can heal.

Such reforms involve some basic conditions. First, relationships have to be established where there are none. When scholars write of the organizational determinants of policy capacity, largely, they are describing the strength of active, learning relationships among policy actors (e.g., Dunlop, 2015; Wu et al., 2015). We have to pay attention to connectedness, especially when broad swaths of a community are excluded from policymaking. Or when divisions prevent active relational transactions across the divide. If the last decade has provided any lessons in governance, it is that the polarization of a polity (which involves seclusion of groups one from another such that they do not interrelate) hinders policymaking, whether we are concerned with divisions over Brexit in the United Kingdom, the red-blue divide in the United States, pro- or anti-monarchism in Thailand, partisan politics in Venezuela, or other battlegrounds. Division is often fueled by social media, which allows groups to self-ensconce in "echo chambers" that serve to isolate groups from one another (Jamieson and Cappella, 2008). In these situations, one group never really encounters the authentic other, and bridging relationships are needed.

Secondly, relationships need to be equitable and responsive to the needs of the other, as the considerable literature on power and politics has shown us. Perverse policies have resulted from arrangements that systematically disenfranchised certain groups in relationships of domination, whether one thinks of the historical marginalization of Native Americans in the United States, Aborigines in Australia, Muslims in India, or other disenfranchisement. And reflect on how many of these, and other structured racial and socio-cultural divisions, are still active today. Policy occurs within and through these relational systems. Moreover, truly responsive policymaking cannot occur without, at the same time, beginning to address these broken (and institutionalized) relationships.

Relationality is not just a phenomenon to be described, it can also be an ethic for reforming policies and institutions. Take, for example, suggestions for a more "relational state" that involves, first, the co-production of policies with the governed and, second, fostering relationships among the governed (Cooke and Muir, 2012). These scholars point to the limitations of reforms undertaken as part of the "new public management" initiatives, with their focus on setting targets and using markets to introduce competition for social and health services (see also Mulgan, 2012). They point out that these initiatives have ignored the health of the relationships between government and citizenry that are needed for policy to be more responsive to the latter's needs and preferences. Creating new forums for engagement among multiple publics comports with the idea of democratizing policy deliberation. With a sufficiently engaged public, policy might to some extent be thought of as co-designed, instead of constructed within centers of authority (Evans and Terrey, 2016). The relational dimensions of governance need to be foregrounded – that is, the government and its leaders need to become "virtuous hearers" amplifying the voice of the governed (Hand, 2021).

The aim of building more active and equitable relationships between multiple publics may require crafting new institutions and bodies for governance. As an example, in 1970, Bangladesh suffered the most tragic calamity in recorded history, as Cyclone Bhola swept through its southern coast and took the lives of more than 300,000 people. In the wake of the tragedy, the government sought to create a new agency tasked with disaster risk reduction. At the same time, it had to deal with limitations in budget and staffing. The solution, which evolved over decades, was to create a new program whose workforce consisted largely of community resident volunteers working with a small department staff. The result was the Cyclone Preparedness Programme which today draws more than 90 percent of its staff from community volunteers, with women comprising about half of the volunteer corps (ICCCAD, 2022). It is a unique institutional design based on fostering new networks of relationships around collaborative governance. This intricate interrelationship between government and community is thought to be among the factors that have helped reduce the toll of disasters by a thousand-fold (Haque et al., 2012).

An important aspect of relational governance consists in engaging community in building working ties with government. The first rationale for this is to strengthen social capital to the point that greater participation of community in policy is possible. But another reason for it is to ensure that everyone in a community is connected to a social network, that no one is an island. In some communities in India, isolation has been a factor in the vulnerability of many lower-income residents to poor health. The response was to deputize more than three million females, referred to as Accredited Social Health Activists (ASHA), who would go door-to-door to ensure that no one was left out of the primary healthcare initiative, something especially crucial in rural areas where restrictions around caste and purdah may be practiced. The ASHA workers would later prove to be a quickly mobilized workforce, when COVID-19 struck

(Balachandran, 2021). And, so, one basic relational prescription begins with assessing whether any needed ties are missing, and ensuring that no one is disconnected who should not and does not want to be.

Policy reform can include measures aimed at strengthening relationships among policy actors. In the case of the social services voucher in Hong Kong, discussed earlier, one of the recommendations that came out of the study was to add individualized case management to the program (Kan, 2022). The idea is that each client would have a dedicated case manager, who then ensures that the client interfaces smoothly with different providers and professionals. The case worker is essentially a "relationship facilitator" who can orchestrate these interactions, ensuring that no one is left alone.

Is it possible to create diagnostics for assessing relationship? Can we gauge the relational along some spectrum between that which empowers and that which corrupts? In a sense, social network analysis is all about assessing connectedness – that is, the presence and absence of ties. In some cases, it may be clear that a needed connection between policy actors is missing or active, adverse, or beneficial. But beyond this, this is yet another open question. Relationships are complex phenomena; they are the things that they are, and assessing them is not a simple valuation exercise.

Let us briefly return to the extended case study of the new voucher program in Hong Kong. The analysis in the previous section examined how relational factors were key to understanding voucher utilization and non-utilization. It would make sense if some of the resulting recommendations (for improving the program) were relational in nature as well. Interviews suggested that professionals could have an important role to play in managing relationships around the client. This idea became clearer in subsequent interviews with the professionals themselves (Kan, 2022). Social workers, for example, could pay closer focus on the "demand" side and help better attune policies to the needs of the public (Yu et al., 2021). What professional workers can do, for example, is to provide information about the CCSV, give guidance and advice on service selection, and assist clients to gain familiarity with service units, all these enabling clients to make informed service choices (Prgomet et al., 2017).

Policymakers adopted a so-called strengths-based approach, in which professional workers would shift the decision-making authority to seniors (KPMG, 2012; Ruggiano, 2012) and empower them to make informed choices on service selection according to their own needs (Fotoukian et al., 2014). The case study illustrates how this requires more, not less, of relationships between clients and agencies. However, with the current CCSV program, the responsible social workers are largely unable to take up the role to educate, advocate, and empower clients in making the informed choices during the decision-making process, mostly because of time and resource constraints and the fact that such duties laid outside their formal scope of work. This is a consequence of the lack of attention to relational dimensions of policy.

The recommendation of individualized case management, which emerged from the analysis of the CCSV program, led to a focus group among social work and health professionals. These provided finer details on what an individualized program might look like. The research suggests that a group of well-trained professional workers, who are familiar with the health and social care systems, could work independently to coordinate different services with the participation of the older client. With this in mind, the focus group participants recommended the development of a comprehensive case management model, as described in the interview quotations below.

Dai [female, social worker, service provider]

> "Besides giving information, the responsible social worker can just do a little bit more to help the older people, especially for those without family, in service selection, since it is quite difficult for older people to understand the CCSV mechanism and service content. And also, it is almost impossible for older people to visit the service units alone for service selection. Therefore, the responsible social worker should accompany older people to visit the service units or mobilize volunteers to do so, and also give older people more advices based on their needs."

Chow [female, social worker, service provider]

> "The responsible social workers should facilitate the older people to choose the service which is most suitable for their needs, or even discuss with the older people and family members whether the voucher system is suitable for older people, or they need other kinds of services instead . . . let older people to make their own choices and decisions. However, the responsible social workers are unable to take up this role due to the existing heavy workload . . ."

Woo [female, social worker, service provider]

> "The current CCSV system really lacks a real case manager to facilitate the service utilisation. In fact, older people need someone to assess their needs, develop care plan and coordinate services for them. Presently, the responsible social workers in the CCSV cannot fully achieve the role of a case manager for some reasons. First, the responsible social worker in the CCSV is too busy to do so; second, the responsible social worker is lack of relevant training on how to perform a case manager role. . ."

As mentioned in the previous section, the lack of certain kinds of relational support can be compensated for by other forms of relational capital. Professional support is a kind of compensating capital that can make up for other deficits or limitations among the clients. Within the CCSV program, a professional worker can balance, combine, and coordinate different relational factors, compensating for the lack of other kinds of relational capital. Supportive professional relationships among case managers, seniors, and family caregivers are key for facilitating effective CCSV utilization. The needs of the clientele are unique and complex; thus, an individualized case management model is recommended. For the policymaker, the recommendation is to formally institute an individualized case management system as part of the design of the CCSV program (Kan and Chui, 2021).

This idea of an individualized case management system stems from the relational analysis shown earlier. As the analysis goes, so goes the prescription; if the analysis uncovers relational issues, then the prescription will logically address the relational as well. An apt metaphor for the case manager might be like that of Bourdieu's virtuoso who, in command of the various resources (or forms of capital) available in a context, is able to coordinate, combine, and manage them to produce actions appropriate to each context (Bourdieu, 1977, 8).

The case management approach has been recommended as a service delivery strategy for aged care in Hong Kong (Chui, 2011; Chui and Law, 2016), though such a program has yet to be put in place (Lou, 2014; Kan and Chui, 2021).

The above-mentioned focus group discussed the merits of having a formalized system of individualized case management. In envisioning the role of the case manager, the participants began describing work that was invariably relational in nature (as suggested in the quotations below).

> "I think case management involves different professionals in a team, such as the social worker, RN, PT, OT or ST to work with a client. The role of a case manager is to assess clients' needs and then allocate different resources for the individual care plan of [the] client. For example, if the client has a medical issue, the case manager has to arrange nursing care; if the client has relationship problems or emotional problems, the case manager has to arrange counselling services."
>
> "The case manager is also a coordinator to allocate different resources or match different services to clients based on their needs. For example, the case manager needs to coordinate different services across different professionals, contact housing department, social welfare department and other social

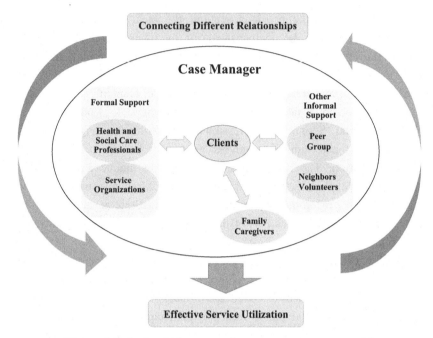

**Figure 1** Relational elements of a case management model

service organizations for clients' welfare plan. For example, some clients need home repair services, the case managers should mobilize some community resources, like funding to help clients to do the repair works; if some clients with emotional problems, the case managers can refer the clients for some professional counselling services."

"There is no standardized definition of case management. Every client is unique. In order to meet the individual needs of the client, a case manager should coordinate different services and allocate different resources for the overall well-being of the client. A case manager should communicate with different people/stakeholders which are related to the clients, such as nurse, PT, OT and family members. So a case manager should be a coordinator and also make necessary referrals if needed."

Figure 1 summarizes the concept of the individualized case management approach. As depicted in the figure, relationships are resources (a form of relational capital) that the manager balances in a way to match the particular needs and situation of each client.

In general, most of the participants pointed out that a case manager should be responsible for assessing the needs of the clients and balancing different resources to make up for deficits. Under the case management approach, a professional worker, normally a social worker or a nurse, takes up the roles and functions of need assessment, care planning, direct and indirect intervention, monitoring, review, and evaluation (Rothman, 1991). A case manager should communicate with clients and their caregivers, coordinate resources and services, and facilitate their decision-making. In other words, the case manager can be viewed as helping their clients "mobilize the power of relationships" (Longhofer et al., 2010, 203). Lastly, the case manager would orchestrate relationships with other agency personnel and service delivery professionals.

The main insight, for this Element, is that these policy recommendations emerge from the relational analysis discussed in the previous section. The analysis showed how users and nonusers tended to differ in the amount and activation of different forms of relational capital. Consonant to this is the recommendation that each individual CCSV client be assigned a case manager (often a social worker), whose role is to help clients tap into and manage multiple relationships. As the case study illustrates, we ignore the relational dimension to the detriment of effective policymaking. This neglect is not surprising, as such analysis requires going beyond the formal outlines of the policy and entering into its inner workings.

Broadly put, a focus on relationality suggests that we put a spotlight on connectedness as an ethic for policy reform. This is most relevant in the case of marginalized communities that are excluded from the beneficiaries of policy, but connectedness is a value relevant to all policy actors. Connectedness is an immediately relevant concept in some sub-fields such as social policy. Another immediately recognized area of application is environmental governance, especially around questions of resilience and vulnerability (vis-à-vis connectedness and disconnectedness, respectively).[8]

## 6 Conclusion

We began this Element with a discussion of anomalous policy situations, when the process and outcome of policy diverges from the intended. This initial focus was a pedagogical choice, as the concepts presented manifest most clearly in these situations. However, we remind the reader that relationality is a condition that is found in every policy situation (non-anomalous or otherwise). It should not be supposed that the relational lens is most useful for situations involving aberrant implementation and rentseeking. While some might want to think of relationality as the "oil that greases the skids," it is more than that. It is constitutive of the life of policy, the fuel that drives the engine.

---

[8] The reader is referred to Lejano (2022) for discussions of relational dimensions of resilience.

The preceding case study illustrates how fresh insights can emerge from a closer attention to the relational. More conventional analyses might lead to changes to the set of rules or resources attached to the policy. Another conventional approach might focus on organizational culture, leading to proposals for retraining of field workers. But the relational view can provide insights into possible reforms that speak directly to the relationships among policy actors – in this case, it is a closer appreciation of how each individual's ability to use the voucher is related to her relational resources, which leads to recommendations for how "relationship managers" can assist individuals. It helps us understand why policy implementation can differ so widely from case to case, even when local rules, norms, attitudes, and resources might not vary. Program challenges might be found not only in the capacities of individual actors but in the connections and interactions among them. Such policy reforms exhibit a degree of contextuality that one may not have conceived of without taking a relational view. Instead of blanket changes in rules, the relational analysis led to a recommendation that would tailor modes of support to each individual client's situation.

With regard to implementation, the relational analysis provides insights that help explain utilization and non-utilization of the voucher on the level of the individual case, which is a greater level of contextuality than one finds in the literature. This is necessary in the voucher example since constraints to effective voucher use appear on the level of the individual client (and, so, is not explainable by typological descriptions of implementation cultures, norms, roles, etc.). A conventional social network analysis would miss these insights, as well, since it matters not just what the client's social network looks like, but how these ties provide relational capital that is crucial for the client to utilize the voucher. In some cases, relationships with peers or other actors can make up for decrements in the person's cultural capital (e.g., mobility, literacy, etc.).

These insights emerge from an analysis, using in-depth interviews, that peers more closely into the relationships among policy actors than one will find in the current policy literature. What primes us to conduct this kind of analysis is an appreciation of the importance of relationality, which understands policies and institutions as emerging from the working and reworking of relationships among policy actors.

As we have tried to illustrate in this Element, relationality is a condition that is constitutive of policymaking and implementation. Relational phenomena can be ignored in policy analyses because they often appear in the "inner life" of policy – that is, in the way relationships steer policy behind the scenes, in ways not acknowledged in the formal construction of a policy. But, as demonstrated in the voucher example, the success of policy can rest on the existence and strength of working relationships among policy actors (including members of the public).

In this Element, we establish several key ideas.

First, we develop the *concept of relationality* in policy life, the phenomenon of how policy is influenced, shaped, and even determined by the working and reworking of relationships among policy actors. Any policy is constructed, interpreted, and enacted by coursing it through a network of policy actors, and their interrelationships (including everyday interactions) will influence the policy. An artificial demarcation was cast, for pedagogic purposes, between the notion of policy as rationality and that of relationality. Of course, in actuality, these are merely shorthand descriptive for the phenomenon of policy, which is not encompassed by any set of representative concepts. Relationality is a feature of every policy context, sometimes working unobtrusively in the backstage, and other times, clearly seen in the workings of public policy.

Secondly, we sketched some outlines of how a *relational analysis* of policy might be attempted. This is an unbounded endeavor, since how we analyze relationships, and how we trace policy designs and enactments to them, is a field of rich possibilities. The policy community is just beginning to construct such modes of analysis. Part of the project must consist in defining, and operationalizing, what we mean by relationship – whether we treat it as a binary variable between pairs of actors, or autobiographical accounts of relationships with the other. Generally speaking, any attempt to trace the workings of policy to the nature and action of relationships among policy actors is relational analysis. We used an extended example of vouchers for social service delivery to illustrate one type of relational analysis and the insights afforded by this perspective.

In the analysis, we saw how the simplest mode of relational diagnosis (i.e., assessing the presence or absence of functioning relationships) already reveals much about policy effectiveness. Going beyond this, accessing the stories that policy actors tell allows us to discover how different forms of relational capital act (i.e., their mechanisms for effectuating policy) and interact, where relational capital often compensates for decrements in other forms of capital on the part of policy actors.

Lastly, we also discuss *relationality as prescription*. In this case, the question is how to reform policy by working on creating, strengthening, and restoring relationships among policy actors (whether we treat these as interpersonal, interorganizational, intersectoral, or other category of relationship). It is often the case that the prescription follows upon the analysis and, so, recommendations can (and should) address relational aspects of the policy situation. In the future, we should assess the relational properties (such as degrees of connectedness among actors) of policy environments.

This by no means implies that we have fully specified a working model of relationality in policy life. This Element is a first step in further developing this way of looking at the world of policy. What we present herein is a phenomenological perspective of the workings of policy, where the primary consideration is attempting a more faithful description of things as they are. And, so, our analysis looks closer at the arena of the everyday, of practice and interaction. Future developments in relational research can also focus on the more formal aspects of policy, one open question being to what extent relational considerations can be incorporated into policy design. Yet another is inquiring into what happens to formal models of decision-making and the policy process when we modify them to reflect relationality. We wonder what would happen to rational choice models when the aspect of relationship, other-regard, and empathy are taken into account (e.g., see Lejano, 2022). What are some relational "logics" that pervade policy processes, and how does awareness of these improve our understanding of implementation? What new approaches could be used to describe and even model the relational? What gains might be had from combining the insights from qualitative (such as narrative) analyses of the relational with the quantitative (such as social network analysis)? And, most of all, what do we learn about policy when we foreground the relational?

While, for the major part of this Element, we have described relationality as the workings of horizontal networks of relationships among individual policy actors, the concept is also useful for analyzing vertical networks that span different "levels" of a policy system – for example, relationships among individuals, local bureaus, state agencies, and national governments. In general, institutions can be described relationally, in terms of relationships among different (vertical) levels of a network (e.g., Ferguson, 2017).

Future work must involve further elaboration of the meanings of relationality and application of these ideas to concrete policy situations. This is not a "how-to" manual of relational analysis but, rather, a primer on the "why-and-wherefore" of relationality. As work on relationality evolves, what is needed are more scholars willing to take up this line of inquiry. But they must be open to departing from convention and doing work that differs from the established themes handed down from august names of policy academia.

We end this Element by invoking the reader to envision an agenda for research and practice. Relationality is an intrinsic property of any policy situation, something that scholars and practitioners have long recognized but have yet to formally study in its own right. Many related lines of work in policy studies have dealt with aspects of the relational but mostly in an indirect way. It is time to put the relational at the front and center of policy work. Our hope is that the policy community can put the concept to use in understanding and explaining the seemingly ineffable nature of public policy.

# References

Akram, S. (2018). Representative bureaucracy and unconscious bias: Exploring the unconscious dimension of active representation. *Public Administration*, 96(1), 119–133.

Alta, A., & Mukhtarov, F. (2022). Relationality as a lens for policy analysis: Preserving harmony in a triangular cooperation project to strengthen gender mainstreaming in Fiji. *Administration & Society*, 54(7): 1283–1304. http://doi.org/10.1177/00953997211073527.

Araral, E., Pak, A., Pelizzo, R., & Wu, X. (2019). Neo-patrimonialism and corruption: Evidence from 8,436 firms in 17 countries in Sub-Saharan Africa. *Public Administration Review*, 79(4), 580–590.

Arnold, G., Nguyen Long, L. A., & Gottlieb, M. (2017). Social networks and policy entrepreneurship: How relationships shape municipal decision making about high-volume hydraulic fracturing. *Policy Studies Journal*, 45(3), 414–441.

Aron, A., Aron, E. N., Tudor, M., & Nelson, G. (1991). Close relationships as including other in the self. *Journal of Personality and Social Psychology*, 60(2), 241–253.

Arts, B., & Tatenhove, J. V. (2004). Policy and power: A conceptual framework between the "old" and "new" policy idioms. *Policy Sciences*, 37(3), 339–356.

Ayres, I., & Braithwaite, J. (1995). *Responsive Regulation: Transcending the Deregulation Debate*. Oxford University Press, New York.

Balachandran, M. (2021, January 8). Unsung heroes: ASHA workers, the foot soldiers of battle against Covid-19. *Forbes India*. www.forbesindia.com/article/the-unsung-heroes-of-covid19/unsung-heroes-asha-workers-the-foot-soldiers-of-battle-against-covid19/65579/1.

Barbehön, M. (2022).Policy design and constructivism. In B. G. Peters and Guillaume Fontaine (eds.), *Research Handbook of Policy Design*. Edward Elgar, Cheltenham, UK, 104–119.

Bartels, K., & Turnbull, N. (2019). Relational public administration: A synthesis and heuristic classification of relational approaches. *Public Management Review*, 22(9), 1–23.

Barthes, R. (1974). *S/Z* (R. Miller, trans.). Noonday, New York.

Bertelli, A. M., Hassan, M., Honig, D., Rogger, D., & Williams, M. J. (2020). An agenda for the study of public administration in developing countries. *Governance*, 33(4), 735–748.

Bertelli, A. M., & Smith, C. R. (2009). Relational contracting and network management. *Journal of Public Administration Research and Theory*, 20(suppl_1), i21–i40.

Bertelli, A. M., & Smith, C. R. (2010). Relational contracting and network management. *Journal of Public Administration Research and Theory*, 20(suppl_1), i21–i40.

Bevir, M., & Rhodes, R. A. (2010). *The State as Cultural Practice*. Oxford University Press, Oxford.

Bevir, M., & Rhodes, R. A. W. (2022). All you need is . . . a network: The rise of interpretive public administration. *Public Administration*, 100, 1–12. https://doi.org/10.1111/padm.12817.

Bodin, Ö., & Crona, B. I. (2009). The role of social networks in natural resource governance: What relational patterns make a difference? *Global Environmental Change*, 19(3), 366–374.

Bohnet, I., & Frey, B. S. (1999). Social distance and other-regarding behavior in dictator games: Comment. *American Economic Review*, 89(1), 335–339.

Bolton, G. E., & Ockenfels, A. (2000). ERC: A theory of equity, reciprocity, and competition. *American Economic Review*, 90(1), 166–193.

Bourdieu, P. (1977). *Outline of a Theory of Practice* (R. Nice, trans.). Cambridge University Press, Cambridge.

Bourdieu, P. (1984). *Distinction: A Social Critique of the Judgement of Taste*. Routledge, London.

Bourdieu, P. (1986). The forms of capital. In J. Richardson (ed.), *Handbook of Theory and Research for the Sociology of Education*. Greenwood, New York, 241–258.

Braithwaite, J. (2013). Relational republican regulation. *Regulation & Governance*, 7, 124–144.

Brentano, F. (1874). *Psychology from an Empirical Standpoint*. Routledge and Kegan Paul, London.

Brewer, M. B., and Gardner, W. (1996). Who is this "We"? Levels of collective identity and self representations. *Journal of personality and Social Psychology*, 71(1), 83.

Bronfenbrenner, U. (1992). *Ecological Systems Theory*. Jessica Kingsley, London.

Brugnach, M., & Ingram, H. (2012). Ambiguity: The challenge of knowing and deciding together. *Environmental Science & Policy*, 15(1), 60–71.

Bruner, J. (2003). Self-making narratives. In Robyn Fivush, Catherine A. Haden (eds.), *Autobiographical Memory and the Construction of a Narrative Self*. Psychology Press, East Sussex, 225–242.

Camerer, C. F., & Thaler, R. H. (1995). Anomalies: Ultimatums, dictators and manners. *Journal of Economic Perspectives*, 9(2), 209–219.

Capello, R., & Faggian, A. (2005). Collective learning and relational capital in local innovation processes. *Regional Studies*, 39(1), 75–87.

Carey, G., Braunack-Mayer, A., & Barraket, J. (2009). Spaces of care in the third sector: Understanding the effects of professionalization. *Health*, 13(6), 629–646.

Carstensen, M. B. (2015). Bringing ideational power into the paradigm approach: Critical perspectives on policy paradigms in theory and practice. In John Hogan and Michael Howlett (eds.), *Policy Paradigms in Theory and Practice*. Palgrave Macmillan, London, 295–318.

Carter, D. P., Weible, C. M., Siddiki, S. N., Brett, J., & Chonaiew, S. M. (2015). Assessing policy divergence: How to investigate the differences between a law and a corresponding regulation. *Public Administration*, 93(1), 159–176.

Case Management Society of Australia and New Zealand. (2015). What is a case manager?. www.cmsa.org.au/about-us/what-is-a-case-manager.

Chang, A. (2021). A formal model of street-level bureaucracy. *Rationality and Society*, 34(1), 6–27. https://doi.org/10.1177/10434631211043205.

Christiansen, T., Follesdal, A., & Piattoni, S. (2004). Informal governance in the European Union: An introduction. In T. Christiansen & S. Piattoni (eds.), *Informal Governance in the European Union*. Edward Elgar, Cheltenham, 1–21.

Chui, E. (2011). *Consultancy Study on Community Care Services – Final Report*. Elderly Commission, Hong Kong SAR.

Chui, E., & Law, C. K. (2016). *Elderly Services Programme Plan: Report on Formulation Stage*. Department of Social Work & Social Administration, The University of Hong Kong, Hong Kong SAR.

Cialdini, R. B., Brown, S. L., Lewis, B. P., Luce, C., & Neuberg, S. L. (1997). Reinterpreting the empathy–altruism relationship: When one into one equals oneness. *Journal of Personality and Social Psychology*, 73(3), 481–494.

Clarke, J., Smith, N., & Vidler, E. (2006). The indeterminacy of choice: Political, policy and organisational implications. *Social Policy and Society*, 5(3), 327–336.

Colebatch, H. K. (2006). What work makes policy? *Policy Sciences*, 39(4), 309–321.

Cooke, G., & Muir, R. (eds.). (2012). *The Relational State: How Recognising the Importance of Human Relationships could Revolutionise the Role of the State*. Institute for Public Policy Research, London.

Craft, J. (2015). Conceptualizing the policy work of partisan advisers. *Policy Sciences*, 48(2), 135–158.

Crona, B., & Bodin, Ö. (2006). What you know is who you know? Communication patterns among resource users as a prerequisite for co-management. *Ecology and Society*, 11(2):1–23.

Crossley, N. (2011). *Towards Relational Sociology*. Routledge, Abingdon.

Debenedetti, L. (2021). *Togo's Novissi Cash Transfer: Designing and Implementing a Fully Digital Social Assistance Program during COVID-19*. IPA (Innovations for Poverty Action). www.poverty-action.org/sites/default/files/publications/Togo-Novissi-Cash-Transfer-Brief-August%202021.pdf.

Dobson, R. (2015). Power, agency, relationality, and welfare practice. *Journal of Social Policy*, 44(4), 687–705.

Donati, P. (2011). *Relational Sociology: A New Paradigm for the Social Sciences*. Routledge, Abingdon.

Dryzek, J. S., & Ripley, B. (1988). The ambitions of policy design. *Review of Policy Research*, 7(4), 705–719.

Dunlop, C. A. (2015). Organizational political capacity as learning. *Policy and Society*, 34(3–4), 259–270.

Durose, C., & Richardson, L. (2015). *Designing Public Policy for Co-production: Theory, Practice and Change*. Policy Press, Bristol.

Dyer, J. H., & Singh, H. (1998). The relational view: Cooperative strategy and sources of interoganizational competitive advantage. *Academy of Management Review*, 23(4), 660–679.

Ellis, K. (2011). Street-level bureaucracy revisited: The changing face of front-line discretion in adult social care in England. *Social Policy and Administration*, 45(3), 221–244.

Emirbayer, M. (1997). Manifesto for a relational sociology. *American Journal of Sociology*, 103(2), 281–317.

Evans, M., & Terrey, N. (2016). Co-design with citizens and stakeholders. In Gerry Stoker and Mark Evans (eds.), *Evidence-Based Policy Making in the Social Sciences: Methods That Matter*. Policy Press, Bristol, UK, 243–262.

Ferguson, N. (2017). *The Square and the Tower: Networks, Hierarchies and the Struggle for Global Power*. Allen Lane, London, UK.

Fernandez de Castro, F., & Lejano, R. (2018). Program implementation and the invisible hand of community: The experience of the conditional cash transfer program in Northern Mexico. In A. Mica, K. Wyrzykowska, I. Zielińska, & R. Wiśniewski (eds.), *The Sociology of the Invisible Hand*. Peter Lang, Berlin, 299–328.

Fotoukian, Z., Shahboulaghi, F. M., Khoshknab, M. F., & Mohammadi, E. (2014). Barriers to and factors facilitating empowerment in elderly with COPD. *Medical Journal of the Islamic Republic of Iran*, 28, 155–166.

Foucault, M. (1975). *Discipline and Punish* (A. Sheridan, trans.). Gallimard, Paris.

Friedman, M. (1962). *Capitalism and Freedom*. University of Chicago Press, Chicago.

Frisch-Aviram, N., Cohen, N., & Beeri, I. (2018). Low-level bureaucrats, local government regimes and policy entrepreneurship. *Policy Sciences*, 51(1), 39–57.

Geertz, C. (1973). *The Interpretation of Cultures: Selected Essays*. Basic Books, New York.

Gilligan, C. (1982). *In a Different Voice: Psychological Theory and Women's Development*. Harvard University Press, Cambridge, MA.

Goffman, E. (1959). *The Presentation of Self in Everyday Life*. Penguin Random House, New York.

González, B. J., & Loza, M. (2016). Opening the archives: Legacies of the Bracero program. *Diálogo*, 19(2), 3–6.

The Government of the Hong Kong Special Administrative Region (HKGSAR). (2021, December 2). Ombudsman examines pilot scheme on community care service voucher for the elderly [Press release]. www .info.gov.hk/gia/general/202112/02/P2021120200295.htm.

Grindle, M. S. (2017). Policy content and context in implementation. In Merilee S. Grindle (ed.), *Politics and Policy Implementation in the Third World*. Princeton University Press, Princeton, 3–34.

Gunningham, N., Grabosky, P. N., & Sinclair, D. (1998). *Smart Regulation: Designing Environmental Policy*. Oxford Socio-Legal Studies, Oxford.

Habermas, J. (1985). *The Theory of Communicative Action: Reason and the Rationalization of Society* (Vol. 1). Beacon Press, Boston, Massachusetts.

Hajer, M. (1993). Discourse coalitions and the institutionalization of practice: The case of acid rain in Britain. In F. Fischer & J. Forester (eds.), *The Argumentative Turn in Policy Analysis and Planning*. Duke University Press, Durham, 43–76.

Hand, L. C. (2021). A virtuous hearer: An exploration of epistemic injustice and an ethic of care in public encounters. *Administrative Theory & Praxis*, 43(1), 117–133.

Haque, U., Hashizume, M., Kolivras, K. N. et al. (2012). Reduced death rates from cyclones in Bangladesh: What more needs to be done? *Bulletin of the World Health Organization*, 90, 150–156.

Harris, L. M. (2021). Towards enriched narrative political ecologies. *Environment and Planning E: Nature and Space*, 5(2) 835–860. https://doi .org/10.1177/25148486211010677.

Healey, P. (2006). *Urban Complexity and Spatial Strategies: Towards a Relational Planning for Our Times*. Routledge, New York.

Heide, J. B., & John, G. (1992). Do norms matter in marketing relationships? *Journal of Marketing*, 56(2), 32–44.

Hill, M., & Hupe, P. (2021). *Implementing Public Policy: An Introduction to the Study of Operational Governance*. Sage, Thousand Oaks.

Hoffman, J. (2013). Theorizing power in transition studies: The role of creativity and novel practices in structural change. *Policy Sciences*, 46(3), 257–275.

Hornung, J., Bandelow, N. C., & Vogeler, C. S. (2019). Social identities in the policy process. *Policy Sciences*, 52(2), 211–231.

Howlett, M., & Mukherjee, I. (2014). Policy design and non-design: Towards a spectrum of policy formulation types. *Politics and Governance*, 2(2), 57–71.

Huff, A., & Cooke, A. (2022). Mixed signals: Understanding the democratic work of narratives in pro-immigrant protests across local policy environments. *Environment and Planning C: Politics and Space*, 0(0) 1–19. https://doi.org/10.1177/23996544221093154.

Huising, R., & Silbey, S. S. (2011). Governing the gap: Forging safe science through relational regulation. *Regulation & Governance*, 5(1), 14–42.

Husserl, E. (1900/1901). *Logical Investigations* (D. Moran, ed., 2nd ed., 2 Vols.). Routledge, London.

Ingram, H., Lejano, R., & Ingram, M. (2014). From discourse coalitions to narrative-networks: Uncovering networks in the deliberative process. In *American Political Science Association (APSA) 2014 Annual Meeting*. Washington, DC.

Ingram, H., Schneider, A. L., & DeLeon, P. (2019). Social construction and policy design. In Paul Sabatier (ed.), *Theories of the Policy Process*. Routledge, New York, 93–126.

International Centre for Climate Change and Development (ICCCAD). (2022, February 10). 50 years of cyclone preparedness: Success in saving lives, but not livelihood. www.icccad.net/the-business-standard/50-years-of-cyclone-preparedness-success-in-saving-lives-but-not-livelihood-over-the-past-30-years-the-number-of-cyclone-shelters-have-increased-from-400-to-14000-but-it-is-still-insufficient-for/.

Jamieson, K. H., & Cappella, J. N. (2008). *Echo Chamber: Rush Limbaugh and the Conservative Media Establishment*. Oxford University Press, New York.

Johnston, K. A., & Lane, A. B. (2018). Building relational capital: The contribution of episodic and relational community engagement. *Public Relations Review*, 44(5), 633–644.

Kan, W. S. (2018). Consumer-directed care: Empowerment model of community care service voucher utilisation in Hong Kong. Unpublished HKU Theses Online, The University of Hong Kong, Hong Kong.

Kan, W. S. (2022). Barriers to an effective voucher programme for community-based aged care: A professional perspective. *Ageing and Society*, 1–20. https://doi.org/10.1017/S0144686X22000502.

Kan, W. S., & Chui, E. (2021). Vouchers and consumer-directed care: Implications for community care services in Hong Kong. *The British Journal of Social Work*, 51(1), 96–113.

Kenis, P., & Schneider, V. (2019). Analyzing policy-making II: Policy network analysis. In Hilde Van den Bulck, Manuel Puppis, Karen Donders, and Leo Van Audenhove (eds.), *The Palgrave Handbook of Methods for Media Policy Research*. Palgrave Macmillan, Cham, 471–491.

Klijn, E. H. (1997). Policy networks: An overview. In W. J. Kickert, E. H. Klijn, & J. F. Koppenjan (eds.), *Managing Complex Networks: Strategies for the Public Sector*. Sage, Thousand Oaks, 14–34

Klynveld Peat Marwick Goerdeler (KPMG). (2012). *Evaluation of the Consumer-Directed Care Initiative, Final Report*. Department of Health and Ageing, Canberra.

Lai, A. H. Y., Kuang, Z., Yam, C. H. K., Ayub, S., & Yeoh, E. K. (2018). Vouchers for primary healthcare services in an ageing world? The perspectives of elderly voucher recipients in Hong Kong. *Health & Social Care in the Community*, 26(3), 374–382.

Lasswell, H. D. (1958). *Politics: Who Gets What, When, How*. Meridian Books, New York.

Lasswell, H. D. (1970). The emerging conception of the policy sciences. *Policy Sciences*, 1(1), 3–14.

Latour, B. (1993). *We Have Never Been Modern* (P. Catherine, trans.). Harvard University Press, Cambridge, MA.

Legislative Council Secretariat. (2012). *Legislative Council Panel on Welfare Services Pilot Scheme on Community Care Service Voucher for the Elderly for Discussion on 13 February 2012*. HKSAR Government, Hong Kong.

Lejano, R. P. (2006). *Frameworks for Policy Analysis: Merging Text and Context*. Routledge, New York.

Lejano, R. P. (2008). The phenomenon of collective action: Modeling institutions as structures of care. *Public Administration Review*, 68(3), 491–504.

Lejano, R. P. (2021). Relationality: An alternative framework for analysing policy. *Journal of Public Policy*, 41(2), 360–383.

Lejano, R. P. (2022). *Empathy and the Commons: A Relational Theory of Collective Action*. Cambridge University Press, New York (in press).

Lejano, R. P., Ingram, M., & Ingram, H. (2013). *The Power of Narrative in Environmental Networks*. MIT Press, Cambridge, MA.

Lejano, R. P., & Shankar, S. (2013). The contextualist turn and schematics of institutional fit: Theory and a case study from Southern India. *Policy Sciences*, 46(1), 83–102.

Leung, H. (2020, March 12). Why wearing a face mask is encouraged in Asia, but shunned in the U.S. *Time*. https://time.com/5799964/coronavirus-face-mask-asia-us/.

Lipsky, M. (1980). *Street-Level Bureaucracy: Dilemmas of the Individual in Public Service*. Russell Sage Foundation, New York.

Longhofer, J., Kubek, P. M., & Floersch, J. (2010). *On Being and Having a Case Manager: A Relational Approach to Recovery in Mental Health*. Columbia University Press, New York.

Lou, V. W. Q. (2014). Case management in community-based long-term care: Good practices and challenges in Hong Kong. In K. W. Tong & K. N. K. Fung (eds.), *Community Care in Hong Kong: Current Practices, Practice-Research Studies and Future Directions*. City University of Hong Kong Press, Hong Kong, 17–36.

Lyotard, J. F. (1984). *The Postmodern Condition: A Report on Knowledge* (G. Bennington & B. Massumi, trans., Vol. 10). University of Minnesota Press, Minneapolis, Minnesota.

March, J. G., & Olsen, J. P. (1989). *Rediscovering Institutions: The Organizational Basis of Politics*. The Free Press, New York.

March, J. G., & Olsen, J. P. (1998). The institutional dynamics of international political orders. *International Organization*, 52(4), 943–969.

March, J. G., & Olsen, J. P. (2010). *Rediscovering Institutions*. Simon and Schuster, New York.

Mazmanian, D. A., & Sabatier, P. A. (eds.). (1981). *Effective Policy Implementation*. The Free Press, New York.

McKelvey, T. (2020, July 20). Coronavirus: Why are Americans so angry about masks? *BBC*. www.bbc.com/news/world-us-canada-53477121.

Millar, H., Lesch, M., & White, L. A. (2019). Connecting models of the individual and policy change processes: A research agenda. *Policy Sciences*, 52(1), 97–118.

Muir, R., & Parker, I. (2014). *Many to Many: How the Relational State Will Transform Public Services*. Institute for Public Policy Research, London.

Mulgan, G. (2012). Government with the people: The outlines of a relational state. In G. Cooke & R. Muir (eds.), *The Relational State: How Recognising the Importance of Human Relationship Could Revolutionise the Role of the State*. Institute for Public Policy Research, London, 20–34.

Nisar, M. A., & Maroulis, S. (2017). Foundations of relating: Theory and evidence on the formation of street-level bureaucrats' workplace networks. *Public Administration Review*, 77(6), 829–839.

O'Toole, L. J., Jr. (2000). Research on policy implementation: Assessment and prospects. *Journal of Public Administration Research and Theory*, 10(2), 263–288.

O'Toole, L. J., Hanf, K. I., & Hupe, P. L. (1997). Managing implementation processes in networks. In W. J. M Kickert, E. H Klijn, and J. F. M Koppenjan (eds.), *Managing Complex Networks: Strategies for the Public Sector*. Sage, Thousand Oaks, 137–151.

Peake, G., & Forsyth, M. (2022). Street-level bureaucrats in a relational state: The case of Bougainville. *Public Administration and Development*, 42(1), 12–21.

Pertierra, A. C. (2017). Celebrity politics and televisual melodrama in the age of Duterte. In Nicole Curato (ed.), *A Duterte Reader: Critical Essays on Rodrigo Duterte's Early Presidency*, Cornell University Press, Ithaca, NY, 219–229.

Peters, B. G., Capano, G., Howlett, M. et al. (2018). *Designing for Policy Effectiveness: Defining and Understanding a Concept*. Cambridge University Press, Cambridge, UK.

Piaget, J. (1952). *The Origins of Intelligence in Children*. International University Press, New York.

Poppo, L., & Zenger, T. (2002). Do formal contracts and relational governance function as substitutes or complements? *Strategic Management Journal*, 23(8), 707–725.

Powell, C., & Dépelteau, F. (eds.). (2013). *Conceptualizing Relational Sociology: Ontological and Theoretical Issues*. Palgrave Macmillan, Basingstoke.

Pressman, J. L., & Wildavsky, A. (1984). *Implementation: How Great Expectations in Washington Are Dashed in Oakland; Or, Why It's Amazing that Federal Programs Work at All, This Being a Saga of the Economic Development Administration as Told by Two Sympathetic Observers Who Seek to Build Morals on a Foundation*. University of California Press, Berkeley.

Prgomet, M., Douglas, H. E., Tariq, A. et al. (2017). The work of frontline community aged care staff and the impact of a changing policy landscape and consumer-directed care. *British Journal of Social Work*, 47(1), 106–124.

Ramesh, M., Wu, X., & He, A. J. (2014). Health governance and healthcare reforms in China. *Health Policy and Planning*, 29(6), 663–672.

Ramírez, V. (2021). Relationships in the implementation of conditional cash transfers: The provision of health in the Oportunidades-Prospera programme in Puebla, Mexico. *Social Policy and Society*, 20(3), 400–417.

Rein, M., & Schön, D. (1991). Frame-reflective policy discourse. In Peter Wagner, Carol Hirschon Weiss, and Björn Wittrock (eds.), *Social Sciences and Modern States: National Experiences and Theoretical Crossroads*. Cambridge University Press, Cambridge, UK, 262–289. https://doi:10.1017/CBO9780511983993.012.

Ricoeur, P. (1988). *Time and Narrative* (Vol. 3). University of Chicago Press, Chicago.

Ricoeur, P. (1991). Life in quest of narrative. In D. Wood (ed.), *On Paul Ricoeur*. Routledge, London, 20–33.

Rivera, A. E., Rivera, G., & Carrillo, F. J. (2021). Urban relational capital and new transaction regimes. In Francisco Javier Carillo and Cathy Garner (ed.), *City Preparedness for the Climate Crisis*. Edward Elgar, Cheltenham, 281–291.

Rogers, S. H., & Jarema, P. M. (2015). A brief history of social capital research. In J. Halstead & S. Deller (eds.), *Social Capital at the Community Level*. Routledge, New York, 14–30.

Rothman, J. (1991). A model of case management: Toward empirically based practice. *Social Work*, 36(6), 520–528.

Ruggiano, N. (2012). Consumer direction in long-term care policy: Overcoming barriers to promoting older adults' opportunity for self-direction. *Journal of Gerontological Social Work*, 55(2), 146–159.

Sabatier, P. A. (1986). Top-down and bottom-up approaches to implementation research: A critical analysis and suggested synthesis. *Journal of Public Policy*, 6(1), 21–48.

Sabatier, P. A. (1988). An advocacy coalition framework of policy change and the role of policy-oriented learning therein. *Policy Sciences*, 21(2), 129–168.

Sau Po Centre on Ageing. (2015). *Evaluation Study of the First Phase of the Pilot Scheme on Community Care Service Voucher (CSSV) for the Elderly: Mid-term Evaluation Report*. The University of Hong Kong, Hong Kong.

Stewart, J., & Ayres, R. (2001). Systems theory and policy practice: An exploration. *Policy Sciences*, 34(1), 79–94.

Stout, M., & Love, J. M. (2015). Relational process ontology: A grounding for global governance. *Administration & Society*, 47(4), 447–481.

Stout, M., & Love, J. M. (2017). Integrative governance: A method for fruitful public encounters. *The American Review of Public Administration*, 47(1), 130–147.

Stout, M., & Love, J. M. (2018). *Integrative Governance: Generating Sustainable Responses to Global Crises*. Routledge, New York.

Trudeau, D. (2008). Towards a relational view of the shadow state. *Political Geography*, 27(6), 669–690.

Turnbull, N. (2006). How should we theorise public policy? Problem solving and problematicity. *Policy and Society*, 25(2), 3–22.

Unwin, J. (2018). *Kindness, Emotions and Human Relationships*. Carnegie UK Trust, Dunfermline.

Van Parys, L., & Struyven, L. (2018). Interaction styles of street-level workers and motivation of clients: A new instrument to assess discretion-as-used in the case of activation of jobseekers. *Public Management Review*, 20(11), 1702–1721.

Warne Peters, R., & Mulligan, J. M. (2019). Introduction to a symposium on development implementation: Discipline, deception, and the relational work of development. *Critical Policy Studies*, 13(4), 370–378.

Warsen, R., Klijn, E. H., & Koppenjan, J. (2019). Mix and match: How contractual and relational conditions are combined in successful public–private partnerships. *Journal of Public Administration Research and Theory*, 29(3), 375–393.

Wedel, J. R. (2009). *Shadow Elite: How the World's New Power Brokers Undermine Democracy, Government, and the Free Market*. Basic Books, New York.

Weimer, D. L., & Vining, A. R. (2017). *Policy Analysis: Concepts and Practice*. Routledge, New York.

Wildavsky, A. (1964). The road to PPB: The stages of budget reform. *Public Administration Review*, 29, 189–202.

Wilder, M., & Howlett, M. (2015). Paradigm construction and the politics of policy anomalies. In J. Hogan & M. Howlett (eds.), *Policy Paradigms in Theory and Practice: Discourses, Ideas and Anomalies in Public Policy Dynamics*. Springer, New York, 101–116.

Wilkins, V. M., & Williams, B. N. (2009). Representing blue: Representative bureaucracy and racial profiling in the Latino community. *Administration & Society*, 40(8), 775–798.

Wilshusen, P. R. (2009). Social process as everyday practice: The micro politics of community-based conservation and development in southeastern Mexico. *Policy Sciences*, 42(2), 137–162.

Winter, S. C. (2001, November). Reconsidering street-level bureaucracy theory: From identifying to explaining coping behavior. In *Annual Research Conference of the Association for Public Policy Analysis and Management*. Washington, DC, 1–3.

Wolch, J. R. (1990). *The Shadow State: Government and Voluntary Sector in Transition*. Foundation Center, New York.

Wu, X., Ramesh, M., & Howlett, M. (2015). Policy capacity: A conceptual framework for understanding policy competences and capabilities. *Policy and Society*, 34(3–4), 165–171.

Xin, K. K., & Pearce, J. L. (1996). Guanxi: Connections as substitutes for formal institutional support. *Academy of Management Journal*, 39(6), 1641–1658.

Yu, S. W. K., Lo, I. P. Y., & Chau, R. C. M. (2021). Rethinking the residual policy response: Lessons from Hong Kong older women's responses to the COVID-19 pandemic. *International Social Work*. https://doi.org/10.1177/00208728211036179. https://journals.sagepub.com/doi/epub/10.1177/00208728211036179

# Acknowledgements

The authors express their gratitude to the editor, Michael Howlett, for his guidance throughout the process, as well as the series editors (M. Ramesh, Michael Howlett, Xun Wu, Judith Clifton, and Eduardo Araral) for their support for this Element. They also appreciate the input and suggestions from three anonymous reviewers. This Element uses case study material from Wing Shan Kan's research, and interview quotations used herein also appear in her publication Kan and Chui (2021).

# Public Policy

## M. Ramesh
### National University of Singapore (NUS)

M. Ramesh is UNESCO Chair on Social Policy Design at the Lee Kuan Yew School of Public Policy, NUS. His research focuses on governance and social policy in East and Southeast Asia, in addition to public policy institutions and processes. He has published extensively in reputed international journals. He is Co-editor of *Policy and Society and Policy Design and Practice.*

## Michael Howlett
### Simon Fraser University, British Colombia

Michael Howlett is Burnaby Mountain Professor and Canada Research Chair (Tier 1) in the Department of Political Science, Simon Fraser University. He specialises in public policy analysis, and resource and environmental policy. He is currently editor-in-chief of *Policy Sciences* and co-editor of the *Journal of Comparative Policy Analysis, Policy and Society and Policy Design and Practice.*

## Xun WU
### Hong Kong University of Science and Technology

Xun WU is Professor and Head of the Division of Public Policy at the Hong Kong University of Science and Technology. He is a policy scientist whose research interests include policy innovations, water resource management and health policy reform. He has been involved extensively in consultancy and executive education, his work involving consultations for the World Bank and UNEP.

## Judith Clifton
### University of Cantabria

Judith Clifton is Professor of Economics at the University of Cantabria, Spain. She has published in leading policy journals and is editor-in-chief of the *Journal of Economic Policy Reform*. Most recently, her research enquires how emerging technologies can transform public administration, a forward-looking cutting-edge project which received €3.5 million funding from the Horizon2020 programme.

## Eduardo Araral
### National University of Singapore (NUS)

Eduardo Araral is widely published in various journals and books and has presented in forty conferences. He is currently Co-Director of the Institute of Water Policy at the Lee Kuan Yew School of Public Policy, NUS, and is a member of the editorial board of *Journal of Public Administration Research and Theory* and the board of the Public Management Research Association.

## About the Series

*Elements in Public Policy* is a concise and authoritative collection of assessments of the state of the art and future research directions in public policy research, as well as substantive new research on key topics. Edited by leading scholars in the field, the series is an ideal medium for reflecting on and advancing the understanding of critical issues in the public sphere. Collectively, the series provides a forum for broad and diverse coverage of all major topics in the field while integrating different disciplinary and methodological approaches.

# Cambridge Elements ≡

# Public Policy

Printed in the United States
by Baker & Taylor Publisher Services